Sorry in advance
for making things weird.

A Disappointing Affirmations Collection

by **Dave Tarnowski**

CHRONICLE BOOKS
SAN FRANCISCO

Copyright © 2025 by Dave Tarnowski.
All rights reserved. No part of this book may be reproduced in any form without written permission from the publisher.

Library of Congress Cataloging-in-Publication Data

Names: Tarnowski, Dave author
Title: Sorry in advance for making things weird : a disappointing
   affirmations collection / by Dave Tarnowski.
Description: San Francisco : Chronicle Books, 2025.
Identifiers: LCCN 2025009303 | ISBN 9781797236902 hardcover
Subjects: LCSH: Disappointment--Humor | Affirmations--Humor |
   Consolation--Humor | Self-talk--Humor | LCGFT: Humor
Classification: LCC BF575.D57 T377 2025 | DDC 158.1--dc23/
   eng/20250325
LC record available at https://lccn.loc.gov/2025009303

Manufactured in China.

Photographs by Dave Tarnowski.
Design by Evelyn Furuta and Nghi To.

10 9 8 7 6 5 4 3

Chronicle books and gifts are available at special quantity discounts to corporations, professional associations, literacy programs, and other organizations. For details and discount information, please contact our premiums department at corporategifts@chroniclebooks.com or at 1-800-759-0190.

Chronicle Books LLC
680 Second Street
San Francisco, California 94107
www.chroniclebooks.com

This is dedicated to the old me.
I wouldn't have gotten here
without you.

Contents

INTRODUCTION

6

DAILY MOTIVATION

8

MENTAL HEALTH

24

LOVE AND RELATIONSHIPS

40

OTHER PEOPLE

58

WORK

72

SUCCESS

86

SELF-IMPROVEMENT

100

GRIEF AND REGRET

114

ACKNOWLEDGMENTS

128

Introduction

Life is littered with a litany of disappointments, and you can find many of them within these pages. Are you sad? There are affirmations for that. Angry? Yup. Hate your job? Other people got you down? Motivation feeling as thin as air? Oh yeah. It's all here.

These affirmations are more than just satire. As my old fiction writing professor once told me, "Allow yourself to suck." And that's exactly what these affirmations do. They make space for the suck in all our lives.

Most positive affirmations leave no room for error. "You are perfect." "Everything is going to be okay." No, you aren't, and, no, it won't. You are a flawed person like all of us, and life can really suck. And that is okay. All we can do is keep trying.

When I wrote, "Only you have the power to change your life. So that shit's definitely not happening," I was acknowledging the fact that, yes, I am capable, but I often opt out rather than in. But often doesn't mean all the time.

Disappointing Affirmations are about radical self-acceptance. The main thing I focus on when writing them is facing up to our shortcomings and the bad decisions we made in the past and will likely keep making, because many of us don't learn from them. We learn how they make us feel or what they do to our lives, but not necessarily how to stop making those terrible choices. I'm not sure I can help others to do things that I personally cannot, but at least we can work on accepting what we can't control together.

This book is divided into topical chapters, so you can flip right to the section you need the most. Daily life struggles. Mental health issues. Love and relationship problems. Other people and their bullshit. Work and all of its annoyances and anxieties. The desire to be a success coupled with the inability to get your shit together. Self-improvement? Ugh. It's hard enough to get through the day, let alone learn something from it. And then there's the grief and regret from all those bad decisions that seemed so good at the time.

There are also little essays that begin each section, where I espouse some of the wisdom I've gained in that topic, such as it is. And as always, the photos were all taken by me.

Disappointing Affirmations aren't for everyone. But for those they are for, they're *really* for them. And I'm so happy to be of service to anyone in need. Even if all that is needed is a laugh

DAILY MOTIVATION

Find
Your
Why

What's our motivation here? If this is the first day of the rest of our miserable lives, what are we supposed to do with it? Will we get to anything on our never-ending to-do lists? Will we go to work and deal with other people's bullshit? Will we use the day to work on ourselves? Or will we decide to just call in sick and hide under the covers?

Decisions, decisions—most of them bad. At the extreme end, each is a new high-water mark on a path to self-destruction. But more often than not, it's one step at a time toward mediocrity and oblivion.

Sometimes it's possible to find the motivation to actually do something important with your life. Something to believe in. And those are the days that make life worth living. As Nietzsche so perfectly put it, find your "why"—a reason to be. Something that makes us feel like we have a purpose. That makes us feel like we matter.

You can do it!

But, you know, you probably won't. I probably won't either. And that's okay. No one expects you to actually do anything with your life. So forget about all that stuff. Do whatever the hell you want.

You've earned it.

My Morning Affirmations

"Here we go again."

"Dear god, why? Why?"

"Please, just make it stop."

"Guess I have to keep being me for another day."

"Shit."

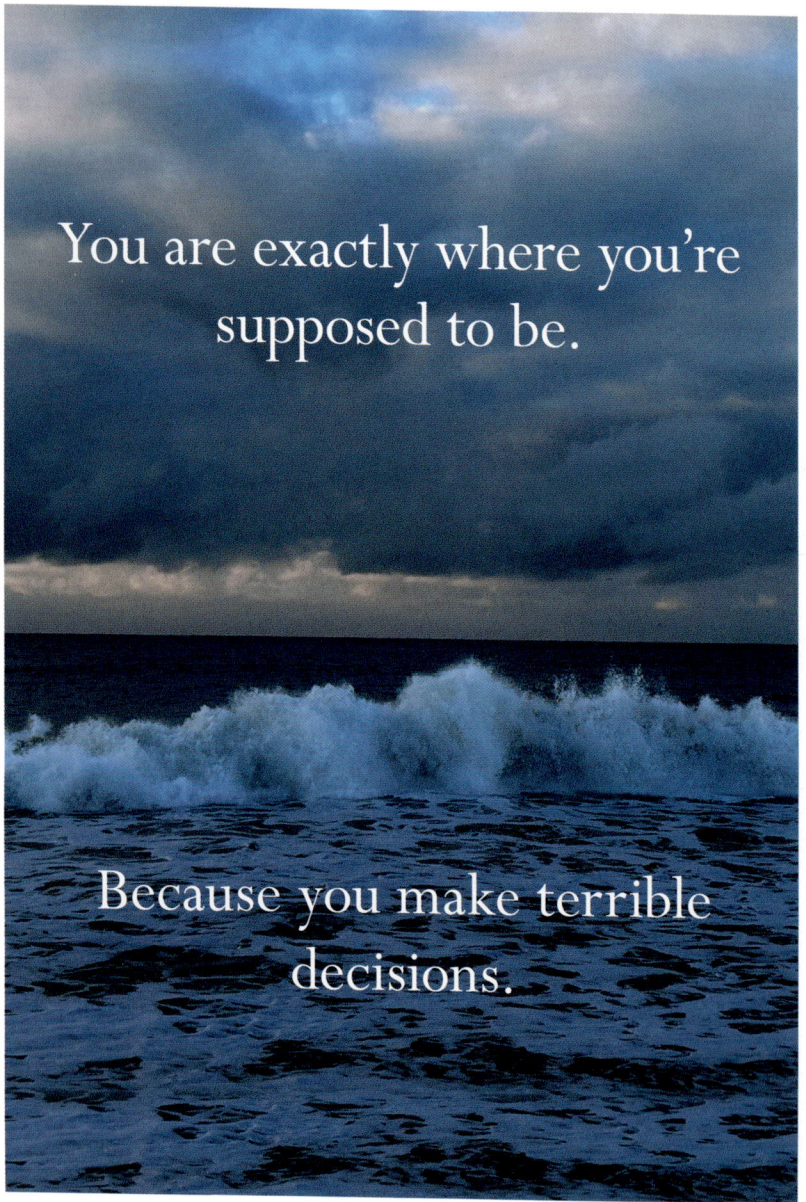

There will never be
the perfect time.

Do the stupid
thing now.

You deserve it.

Just because you can doesn't mean that you should.

But you're going to do it anyway.

Because you never fucking learn.

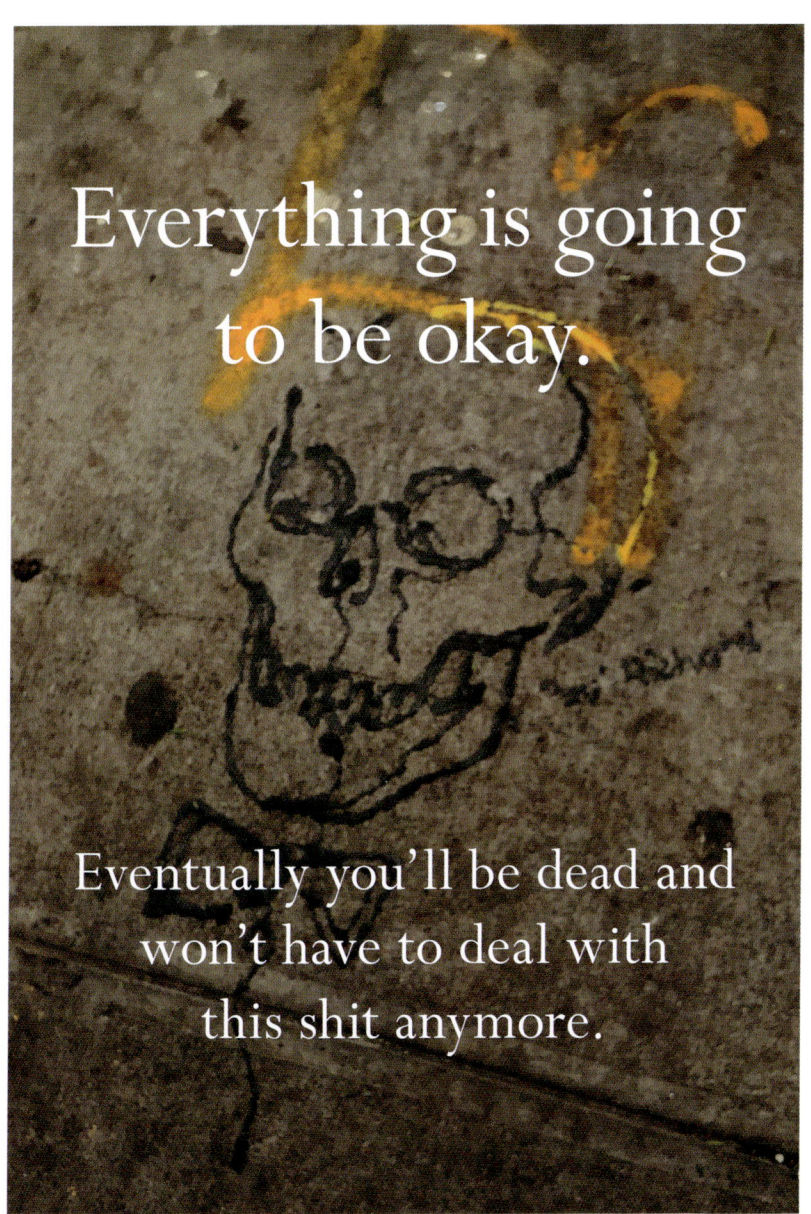

Everything is going to be okay.

Eventually you'll be dead and won't have to deal with this shit anymore.

MENTAL HEALTH

ADHD Vibes

These affirmations would not exist had I not decided to go to therapy. For one, I don't think I would still be alive had I not started talking things out with someone. I'm also pretty sure I would not have been able to make these oftentimes highly vulnerable memes without learning in therapy that being vulnerable is a strength.

I see therapy as a kind of excavation: The more you dig, the deeper you realize things go. There is no "finishing" therapy. No "cure." You just keep digging and discovering. You're not just talking things out; you're developing skills that allow you to better navigate being yourself.

I was diagnosed with bipolar disorder in 2020, but it wasn't until I started making these affirmations that I got the idea there was more to my mental health story. On post after post on the Disappointing Affirmations Instagram page, people would leave comments like, "ADHD vibes." So I talked to my therapist about it, and she tested me, and BAM! I scored off the charts.

It took years for me to find the right treatment, and some days, even with my meds, I still feel like I'm one step away from a panic attack or full-on meltdown. But it's only treatment, not ultimate control—and again, no cure. It's not a death sentence, but rather a life sentence.

But yeah, strangers on the internet diagnosed me with ADHD.

I feel so seen!

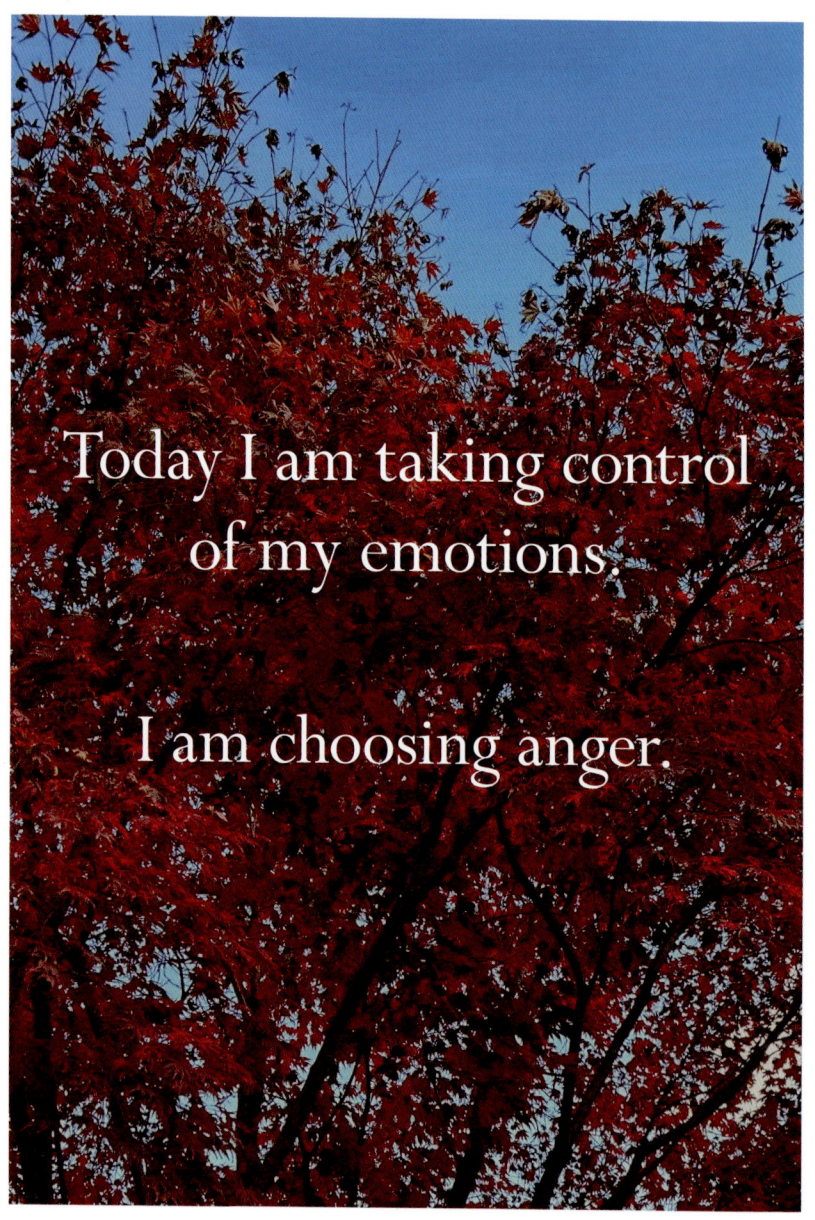

Wherever you go, there you are.

The same bundle of neuroses, just in a different location.

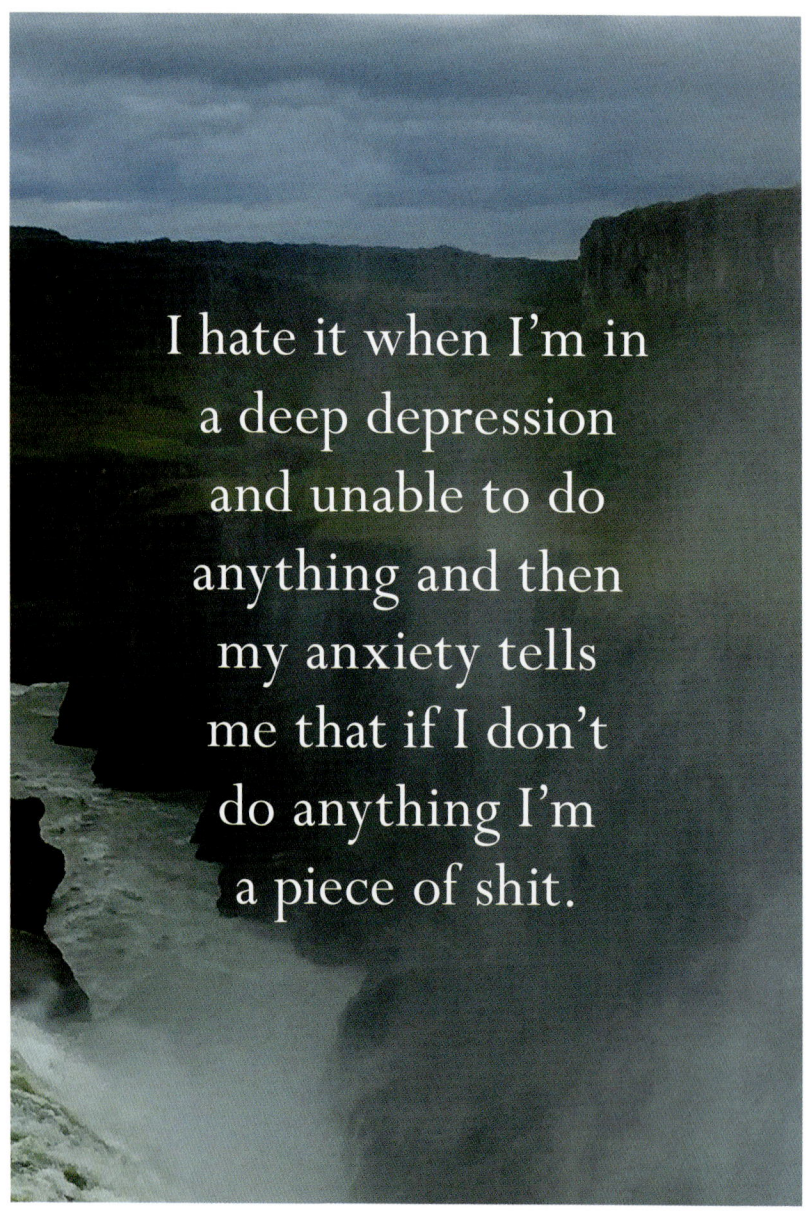

I hate it when I'm in a deep depression and unable to do anything and then my anxiety tells me that if I don't do anything I'm a piece of shit.

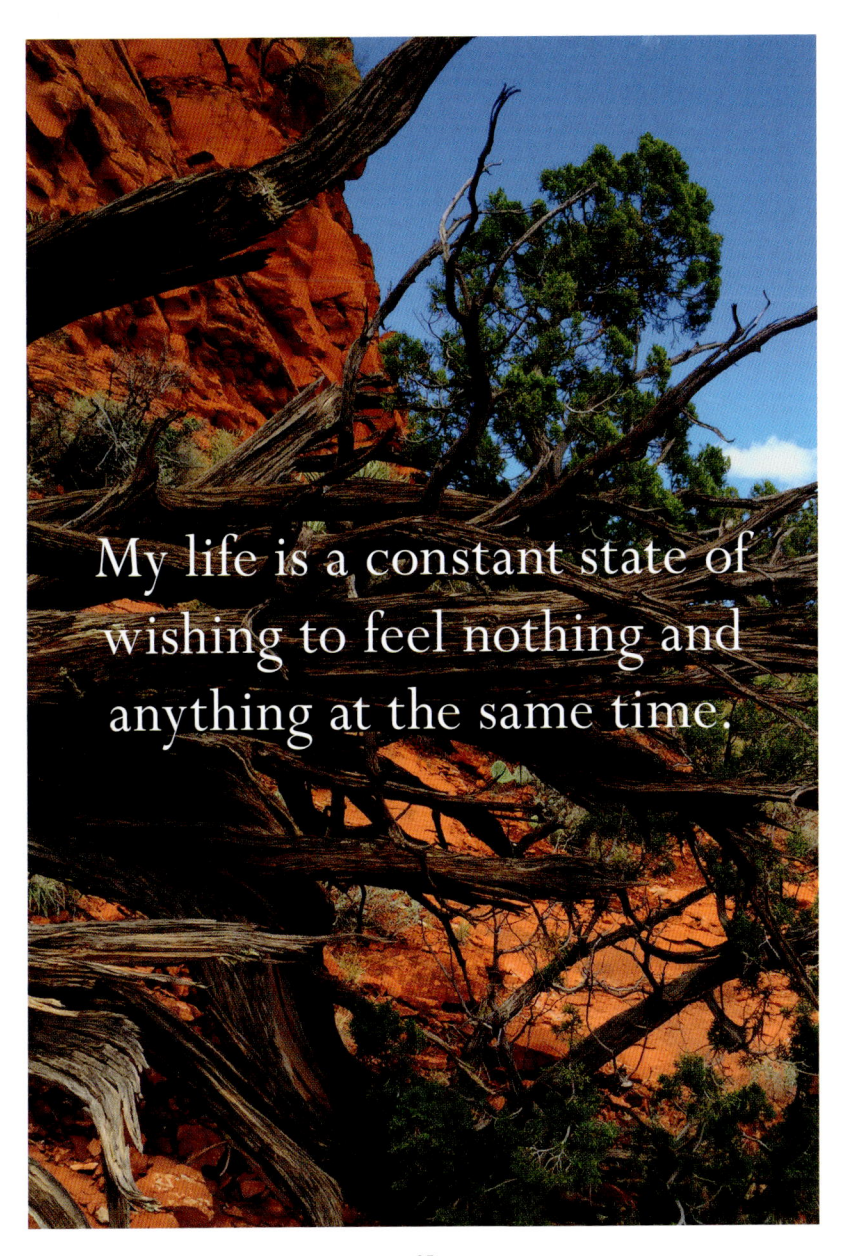

My life is a constant state of wishing to feel nothing and anything at the same time.

Therapy changed my life.

I still do all the stupid things
I've always done, but now
I know why I do them.

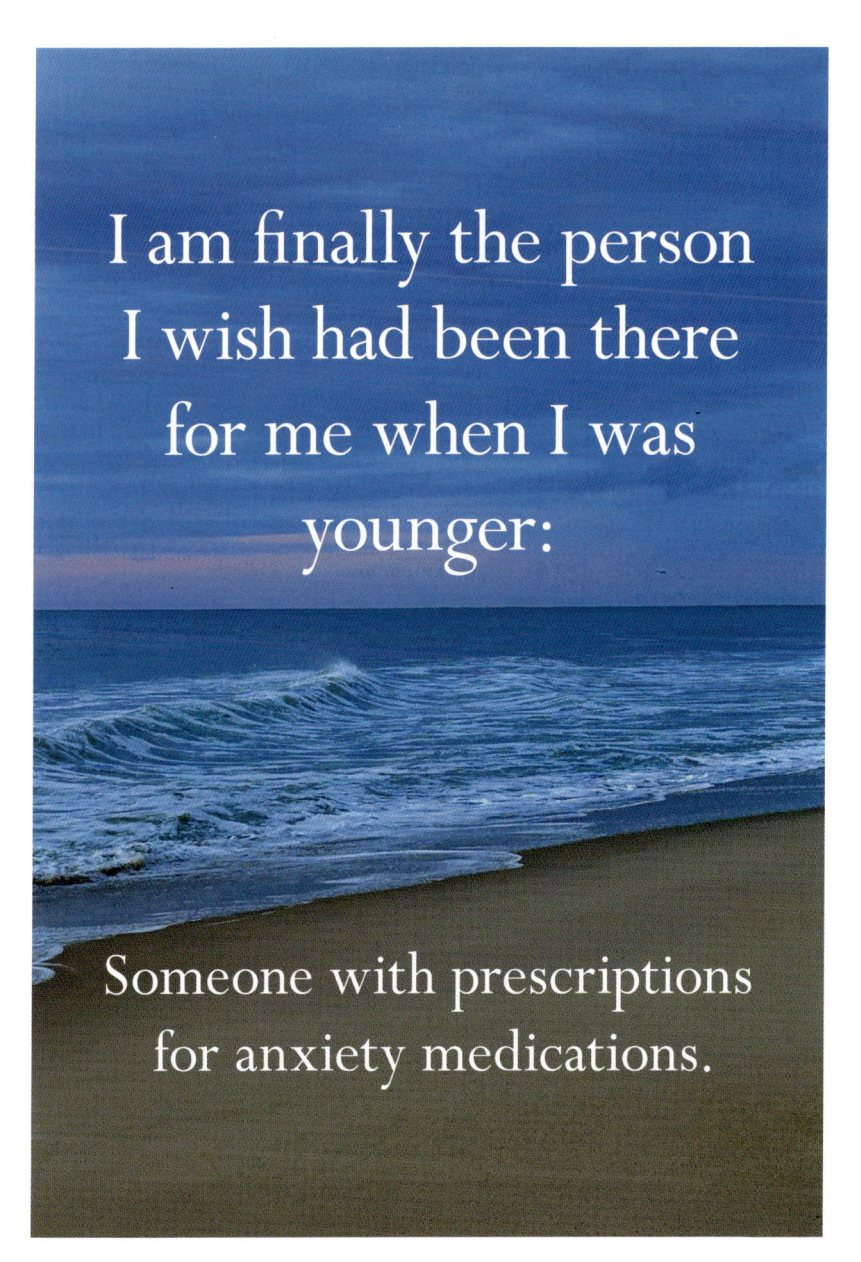

I am finally the person I wish had been there for me when I was younger:

Someone with prescriptions for anxiety medications.

Sorry, I was in a really dark place at the time.

By "at the time" I mean my entire life.

Being dead inside doesn't mean you can't live a happy life.

Just learn to love being dead inside.

Really lean in to it.

LOVE AND RELATIONSHIPS

Love Will Break Your Fucking Heart

There's nothing quite like being in love. And relationships grind that shit down. It's amazing at the beginning—all those yummy hormones and neurotransmitters at work 24/7. It's the greatest painkiller, not to mention hallucinogenic. But at a certain point the drug wears off and all the red flags you ignored at the beginning are on full display. And you spend the next however many years you're together hoping that one day things will feel that way again. But you know deep in your heart that they won't.

There's a part of you that is constantly telling you to get out, that things are no longer good for you. But there's another part in there that has convinced you that the person who exists in your fondest of memories is the same person that is in front of you right now. It's a delusion that is very hard to overcome. Eventually things will get so bad that they'll leave you first, because while you were holding on to a memory, you became someone they no longer wished to remember. And that's love. It always ends in tears.

But maybe that's just me.

I'm sure your relationship is totally fine.

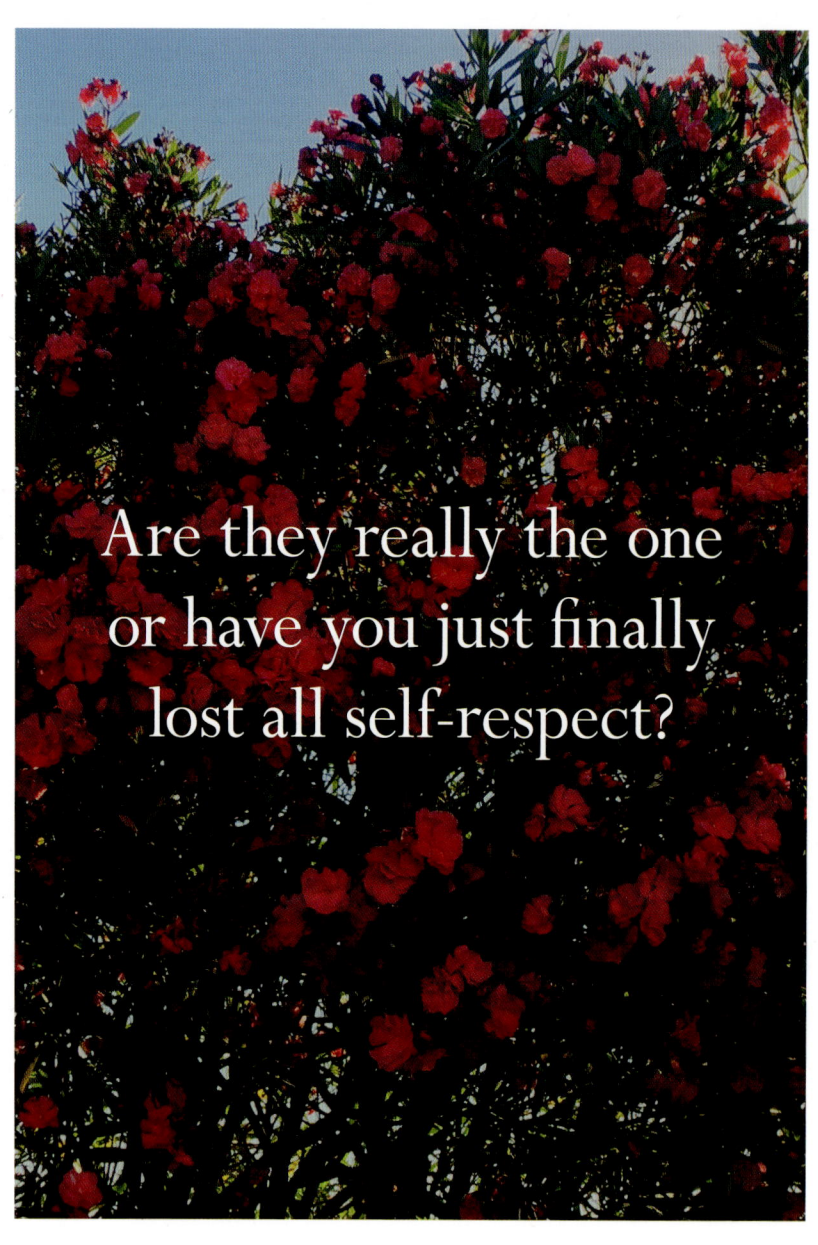

Are they really the one or have you just finally lost all self-respect?

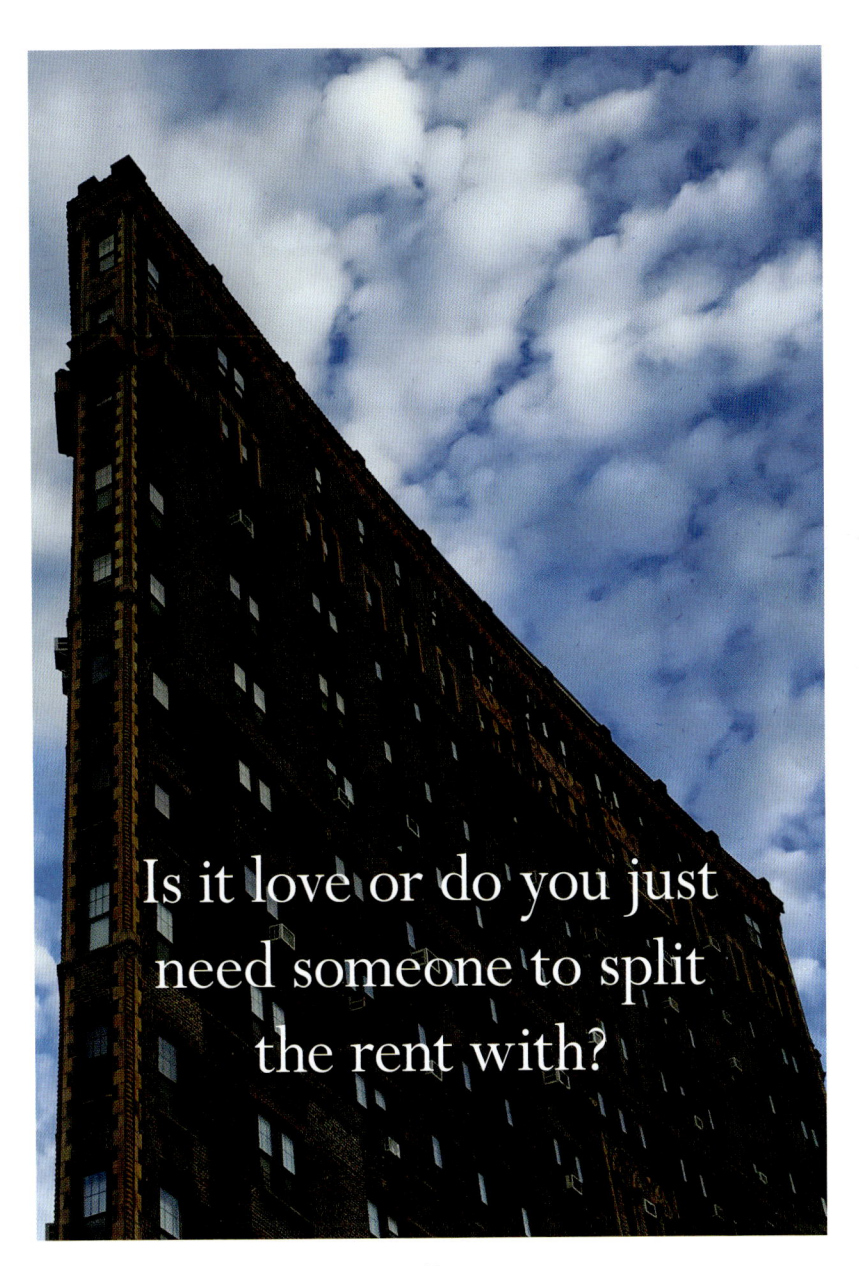

Is it love or do you just need someone to split the rent with?

What's meant to be will find a way.

And then you'll find a way to fuck it up.

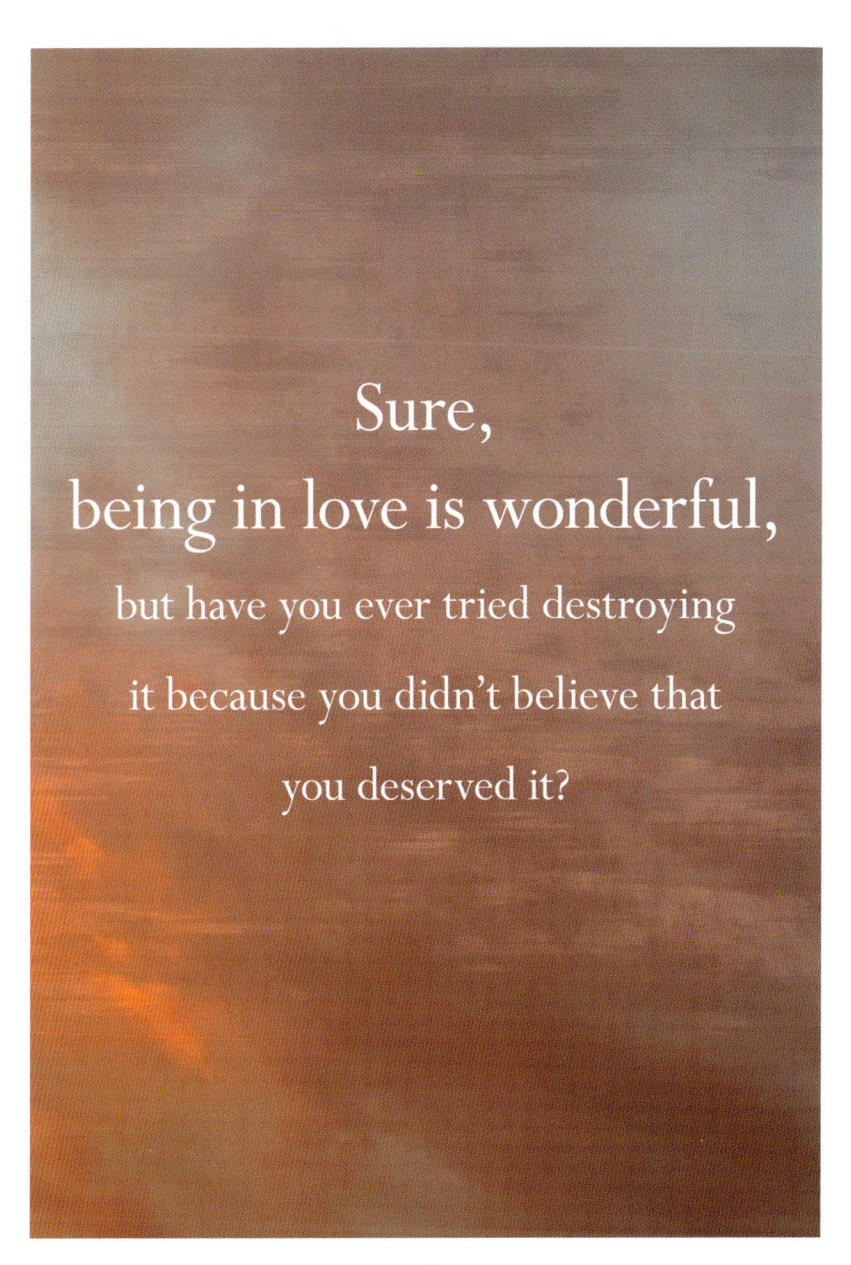

Sure,
being in love is wonderful,
but have you ever tried destroying

it because you didn't believe that

you deserved it?

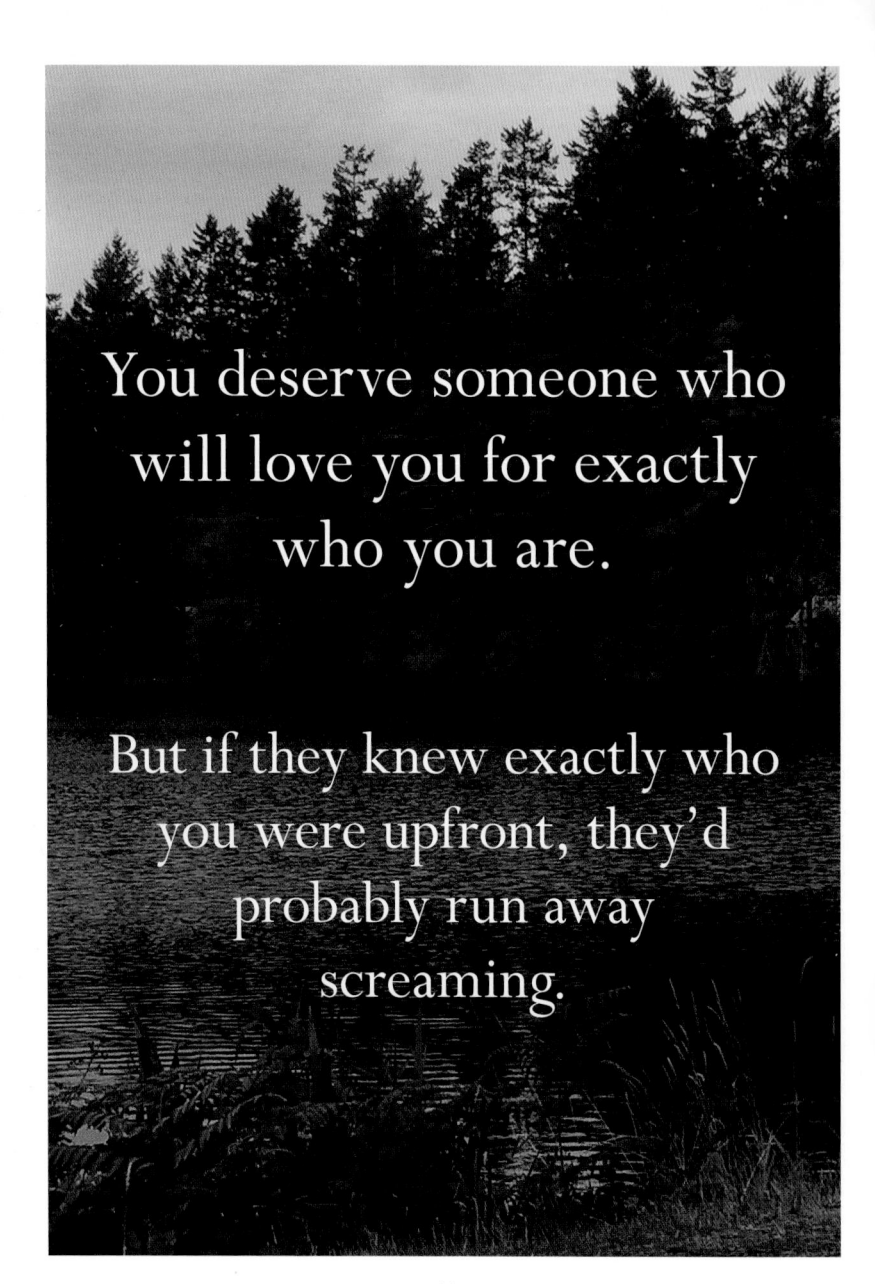

You deserve someone who will love you for exactly who you are.

But if they knew exactly who you were upfront, they'd probably run away screaming.

There's no bond stronger than a trauma bond.

Setting boundaries is essential.

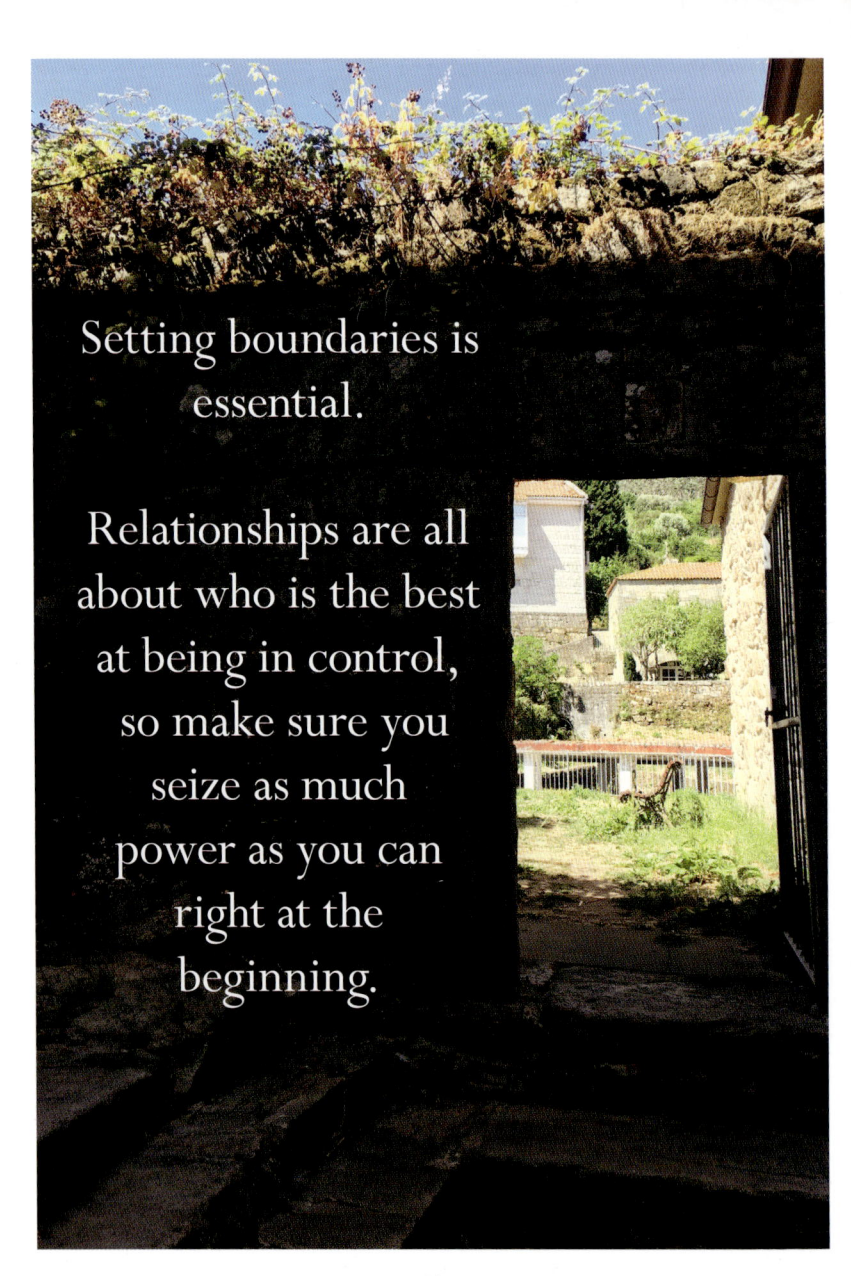

Relationships are all about who is the best at being in control, so make sure you seize as much power as you can right at the beginning.

You deserve someone who gives you butterflies.

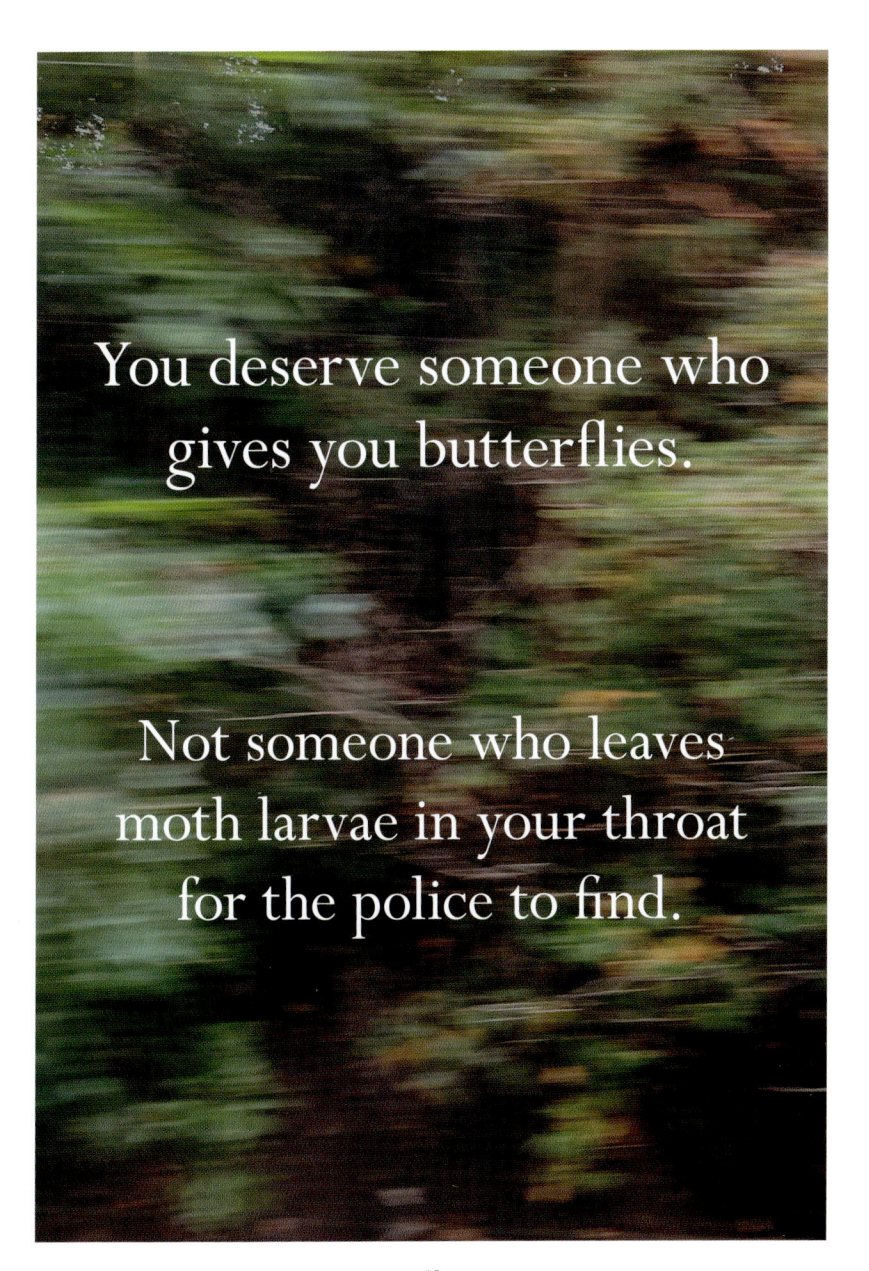

Not someone who leaves moth larvae in your throat for the police to find.

Before you text your ex,
just don't.

Do you really miss them or are you just horny?

Being ghosted is a blessing.

After all, who wants to hear all the reasons why someone they like wants absolutely nothing to do with them?

The biggest red flag is someone believing they don't have any.

I love you more than
I love myself.

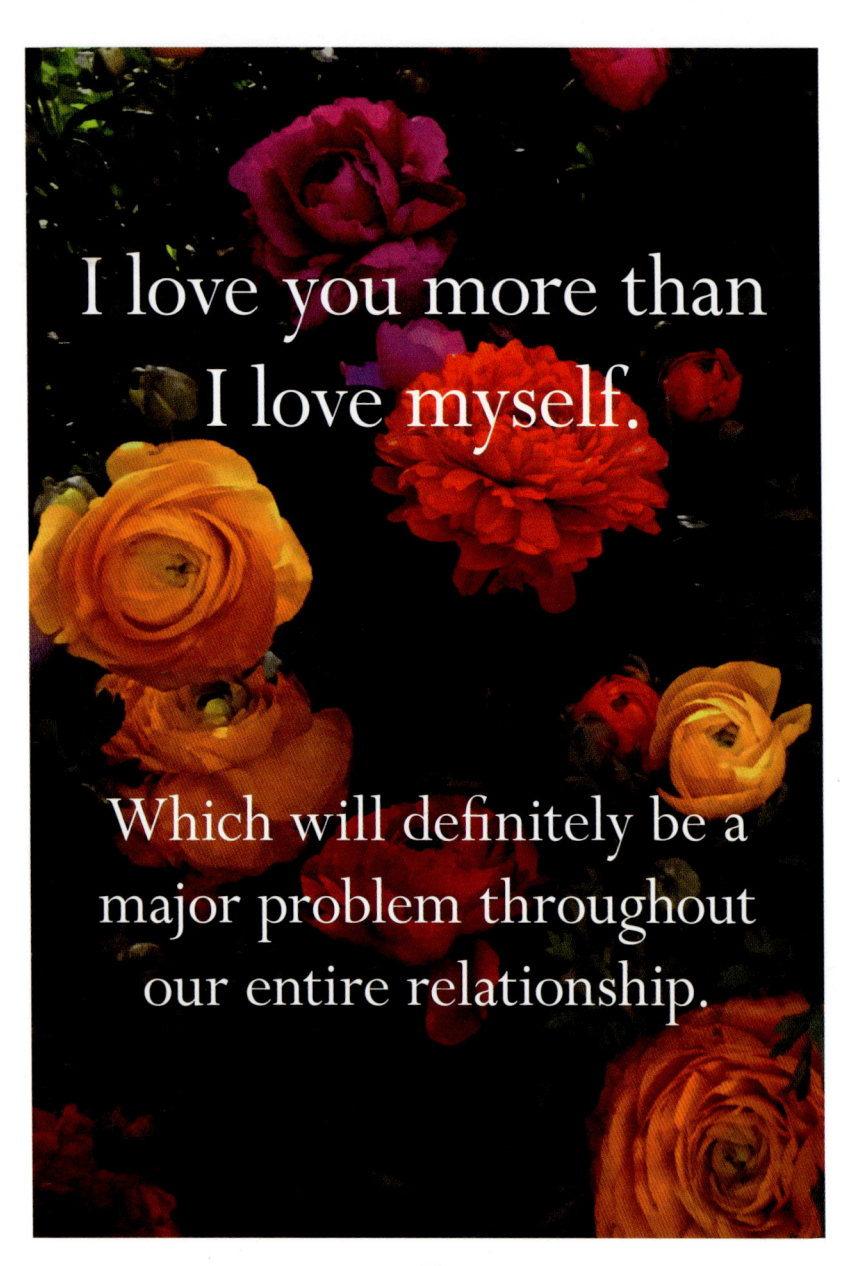

Which will definitely be a
major problem throughout
our entire relationship.

I hate the word "toxic."

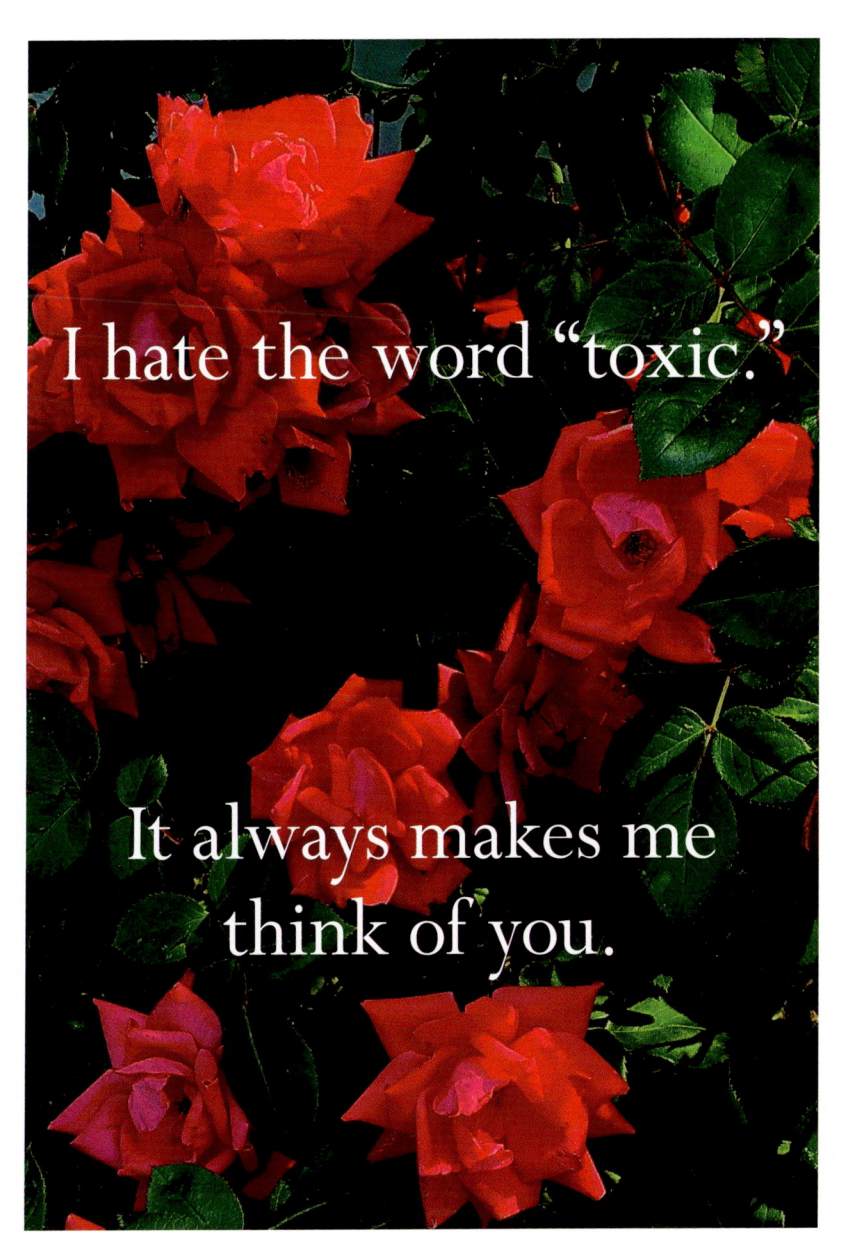

It always makes me think of you.

Why does everything remind me of them?

Move the fuck on already.

OTHER PEOPLE

People Suck

Suck

(Me Dry)

Who would we be without other people? Our family, friends, colleagues, the asshole holding up the line to buy every scratch-off lotto card the store has to offer. All these characters flesh out the stories of our lives. And they can all stay the hell away from me. Text me, don't call. I'm not going to answer because I don't want to hear it.

The biggest problem when it comes to other people is they all have opinions, particularly about how we should live our lives. Sure, often they mean well, but their advice is only a reflection of the narrow scope of their personal experiences. And their fears.

And what would we be without our fears? They keep us in line and showing up at our jobs on time. Some of us spend our entire lives proving ourselves to other people while never really knowing our own self-worth. It's so easy to lose yourself to a constant churn of serving other people and their successes while never truly being a success because you're too busy just doing your job. And then you have to deal with those other people that you're related to, which can be a second full-time job with all the stresses and anxieties but no paycheck.

People are the absolute worst. But then, we're all other people to someone. I know I'm no picnic. Lucky for everyone, I avoid people like the plague.

Prioritize your mental health.

Avoid people whenever possible.

I am choosing kindness over anger.

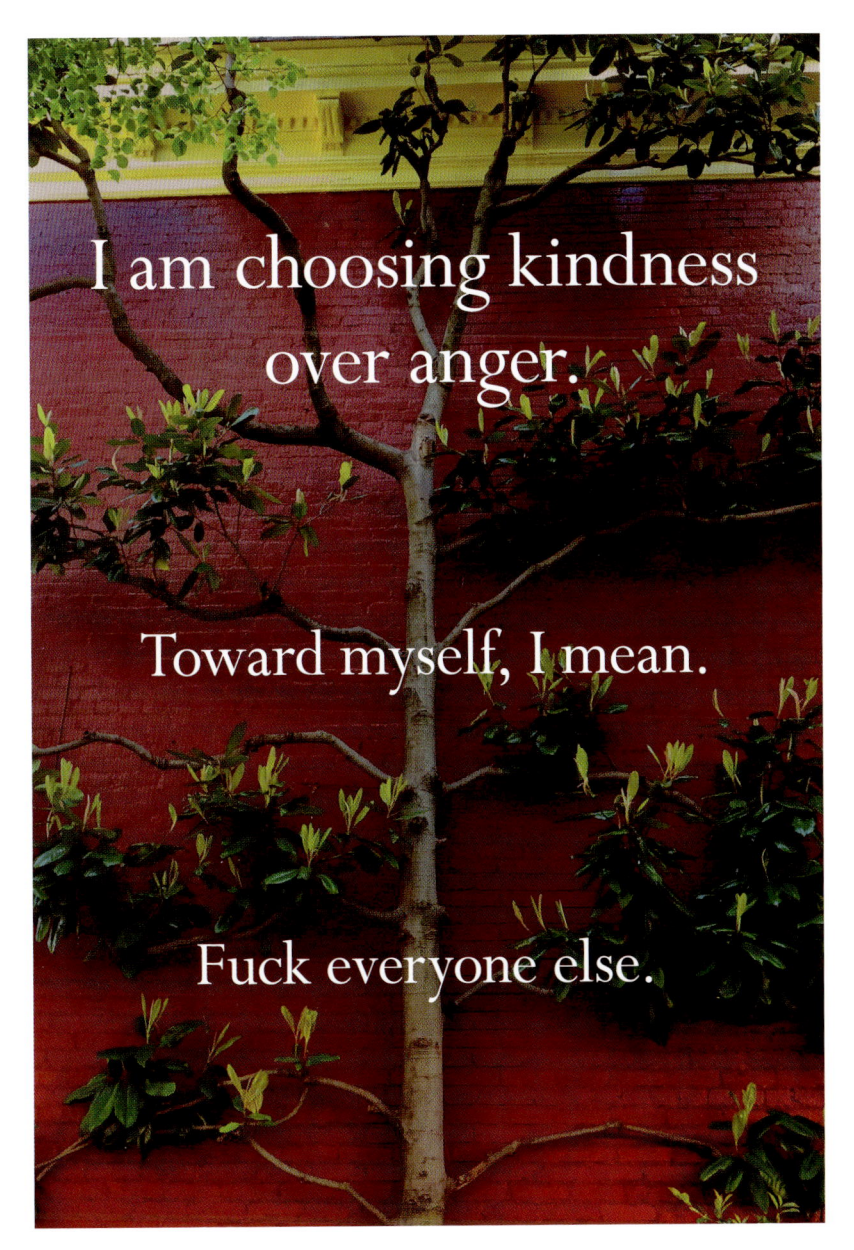

Toward myself, I mean.

Fuck everyone else.

Do something nice for someone today.

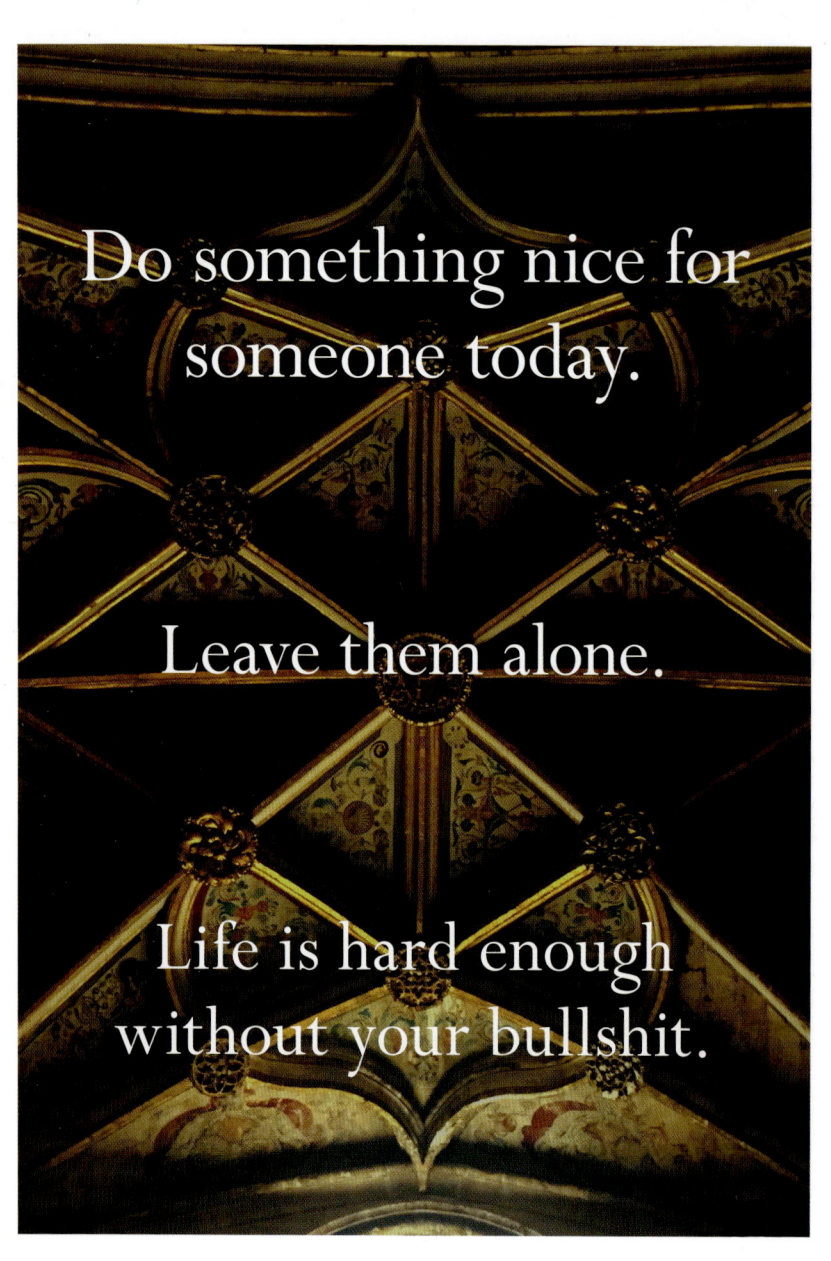

Leave them alone.

Life is hard enough without your bullshit.

Be the energy you want to attract.

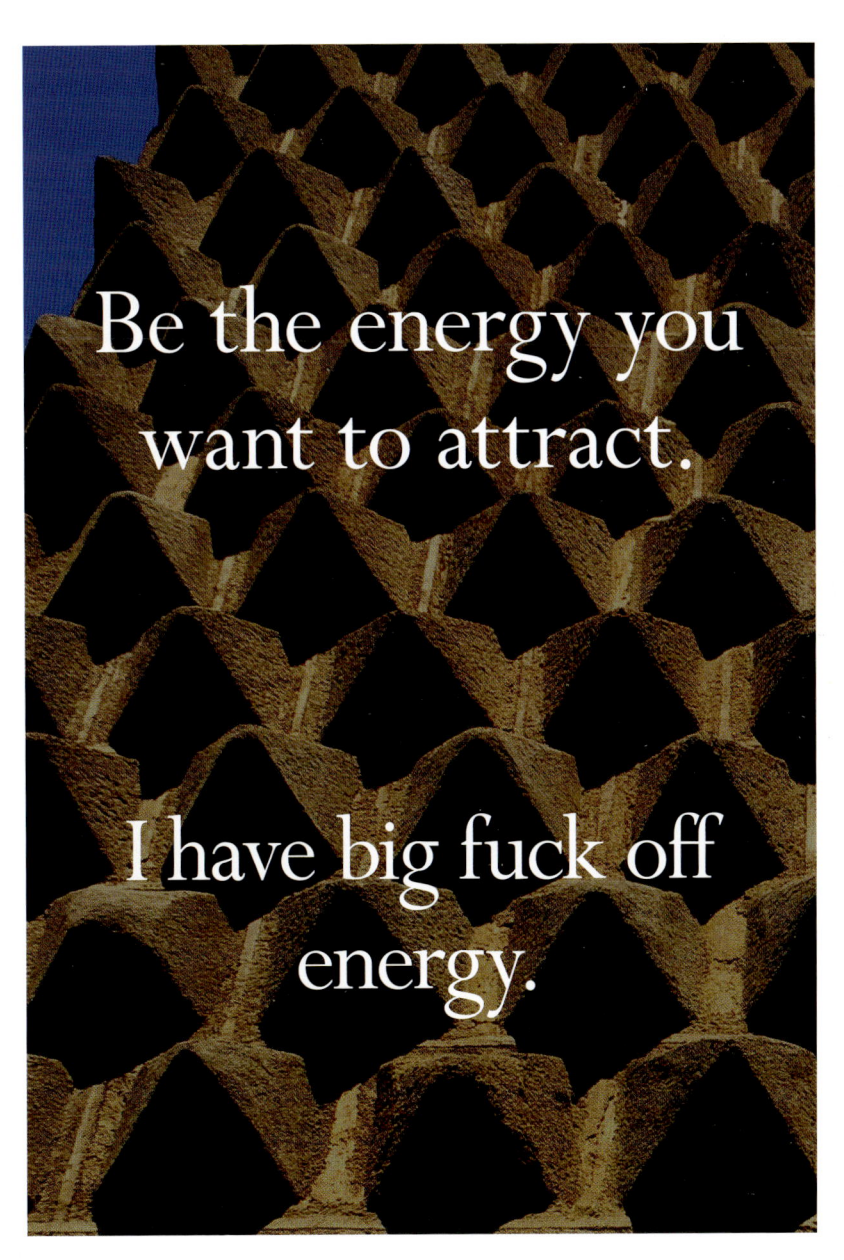

I have big fuck off energy.

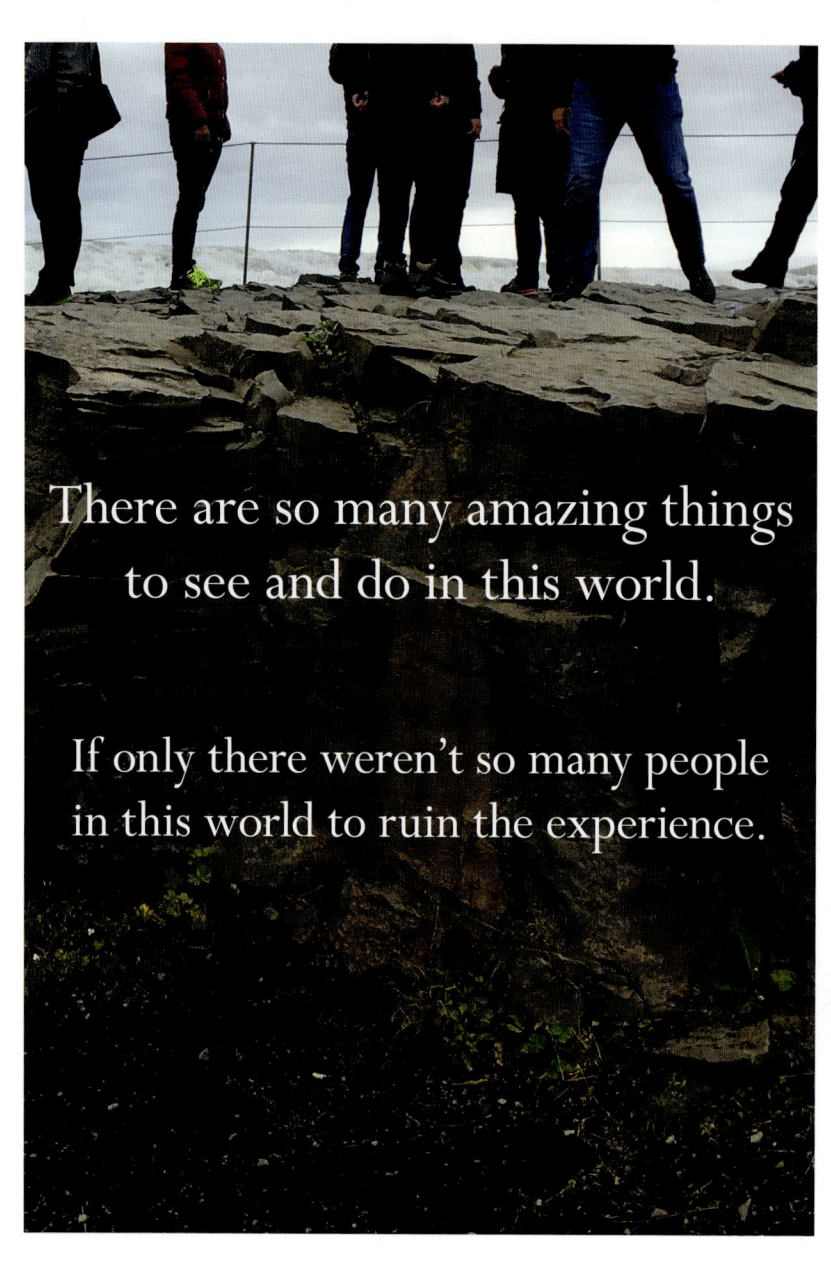

There are so many amazing things to see and do in this world.

If only there weren't so many people in this world to ruin the experience.

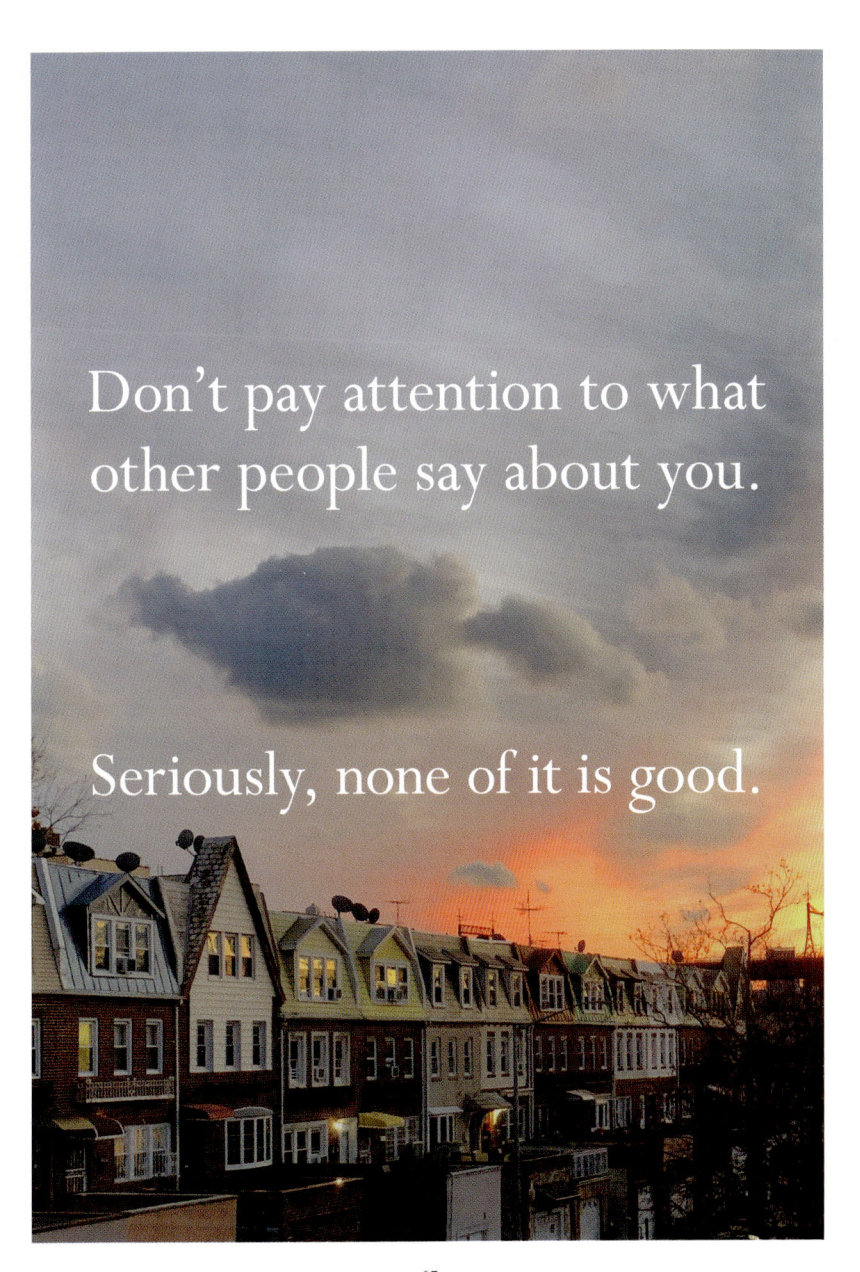

Don't pay attention to what other people say about you.

Seriously, none of it is good.

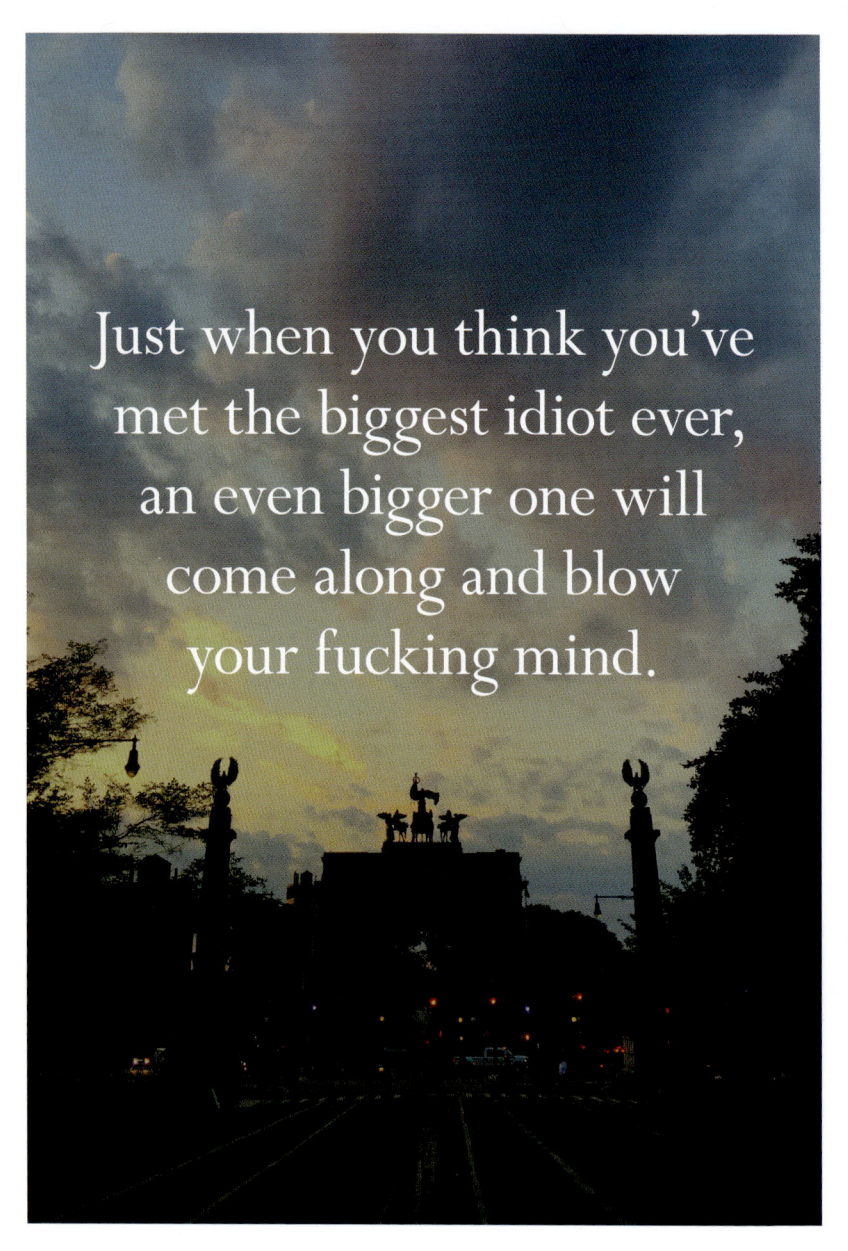

Just when you think you've met the biggest idiot ever, an even bigger one will come along and blow your fucking mind.

People come into our lives for a reason.

Quite often that reason is to shit all over the things we care about and make us believe that who we are is wrong.

Whenever someone asks me
what I want, I always feel
like saying:

"To be left alone."

Always be your true, authentic self.

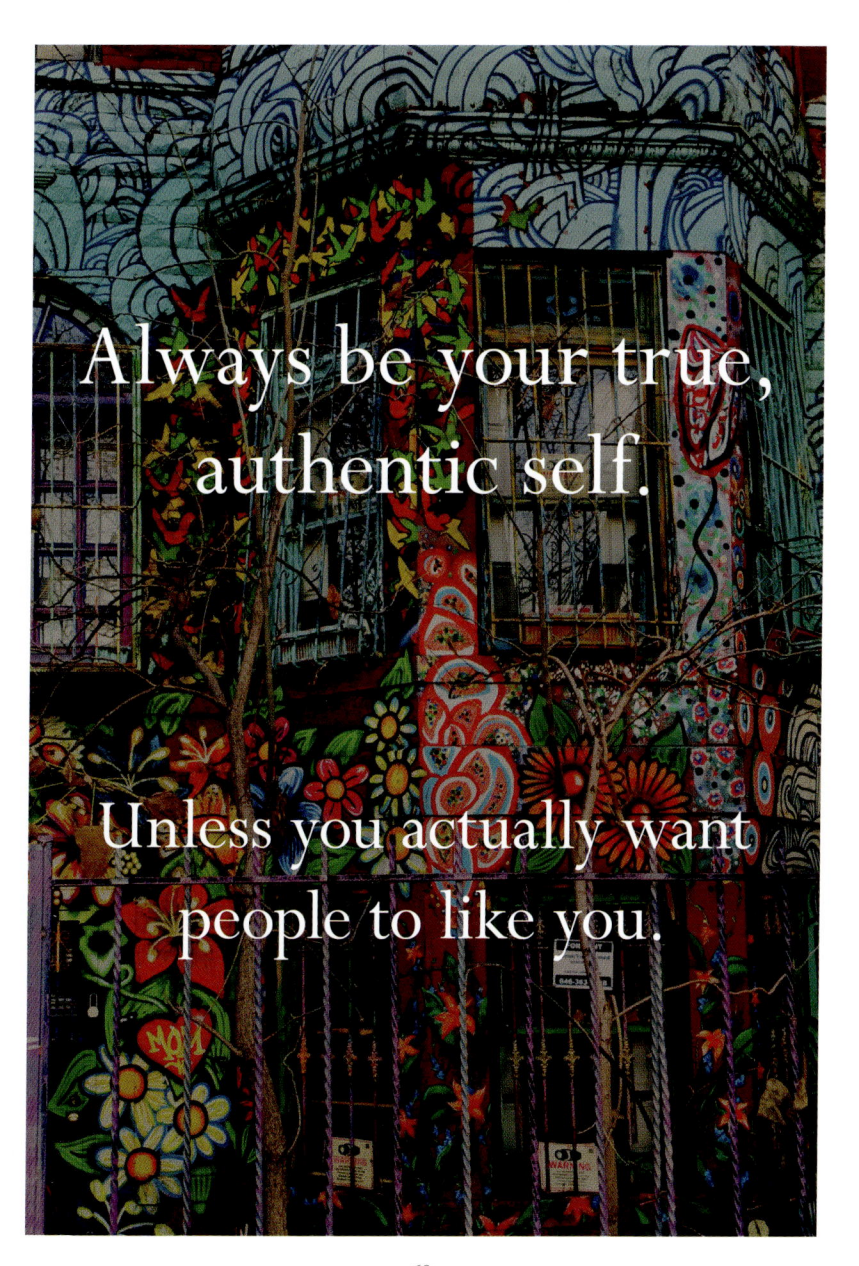

Unless you actually want people to like you.

A great trick for remembering the names of people you meet is to just not meet any people.

You make the world a better place.

Everyone needs someone they can point to and say: "At least I'm not them."

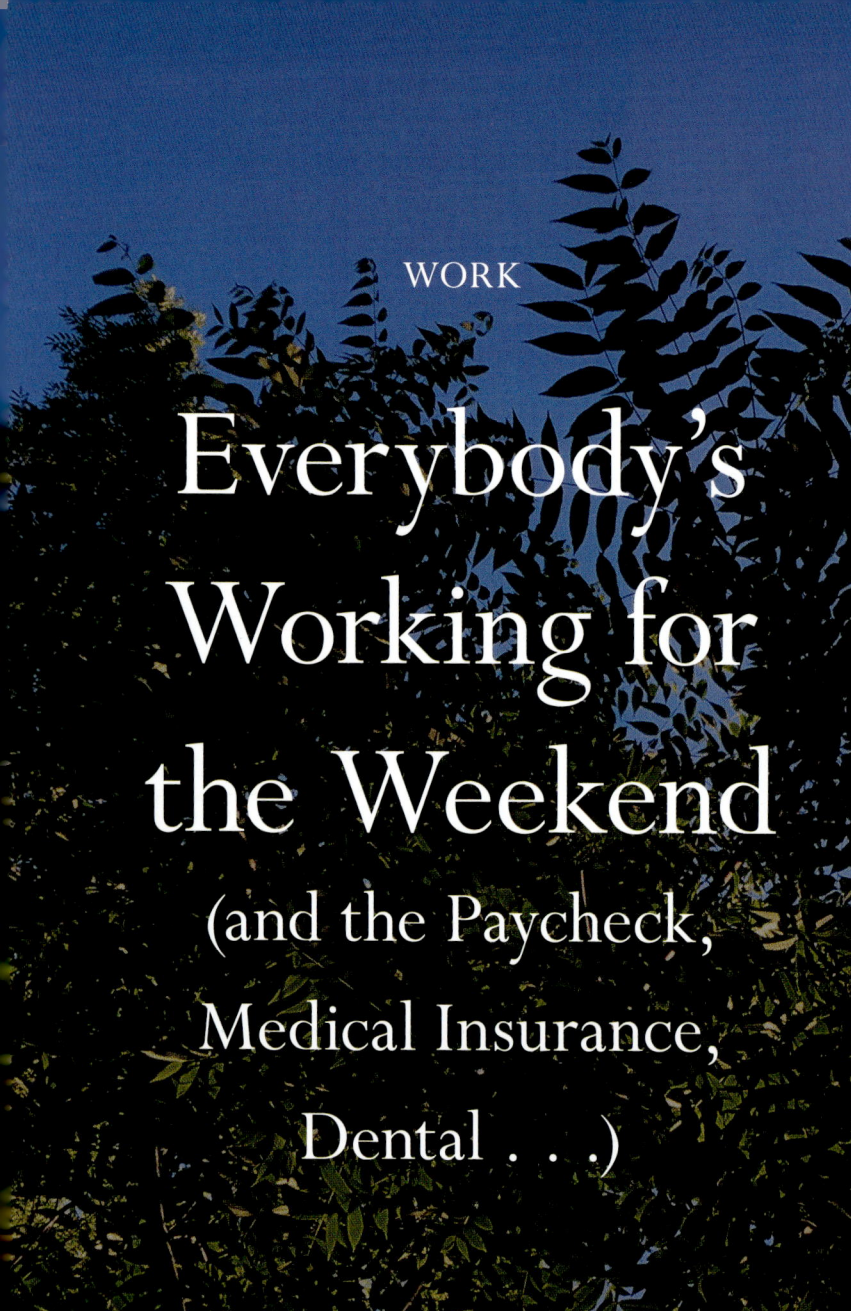

WORK

Everybody's Working for the Weekend

(and the Paycheck, Medical Insurance, Dental . . .)

Waking up for work is the worst. You hit snooze ten times before reality forces you out of bed. It's the last thing you want to do, but it takes money to live. So you stumble through your morning routine, dreading all the bullshit that awaits you when it's time to show up and do your job. You're constantly in panic mode from all the unfinished projects that will never get done because some newer, more important bullshit always pops up, and you really wish you could crawl back into the womb—or into a hole and die.

But no. You buck up and forge ahead. The day has only just begun, and already you want it done so you can enjoy your moment of free time before you have to go to sleep and do it all again tomorrow. And on and on it goes. Weekends are no respite. You're too tired from the workweek to do anything important. Then you curse yourself Monday morning when the vicious cycle begins anew.

Or maybe you actually enjoy your life.

One day you will die.

But for now you still have to go to work.

Each new dawn brings with it the promise of more bullshit to get through.

You got this.

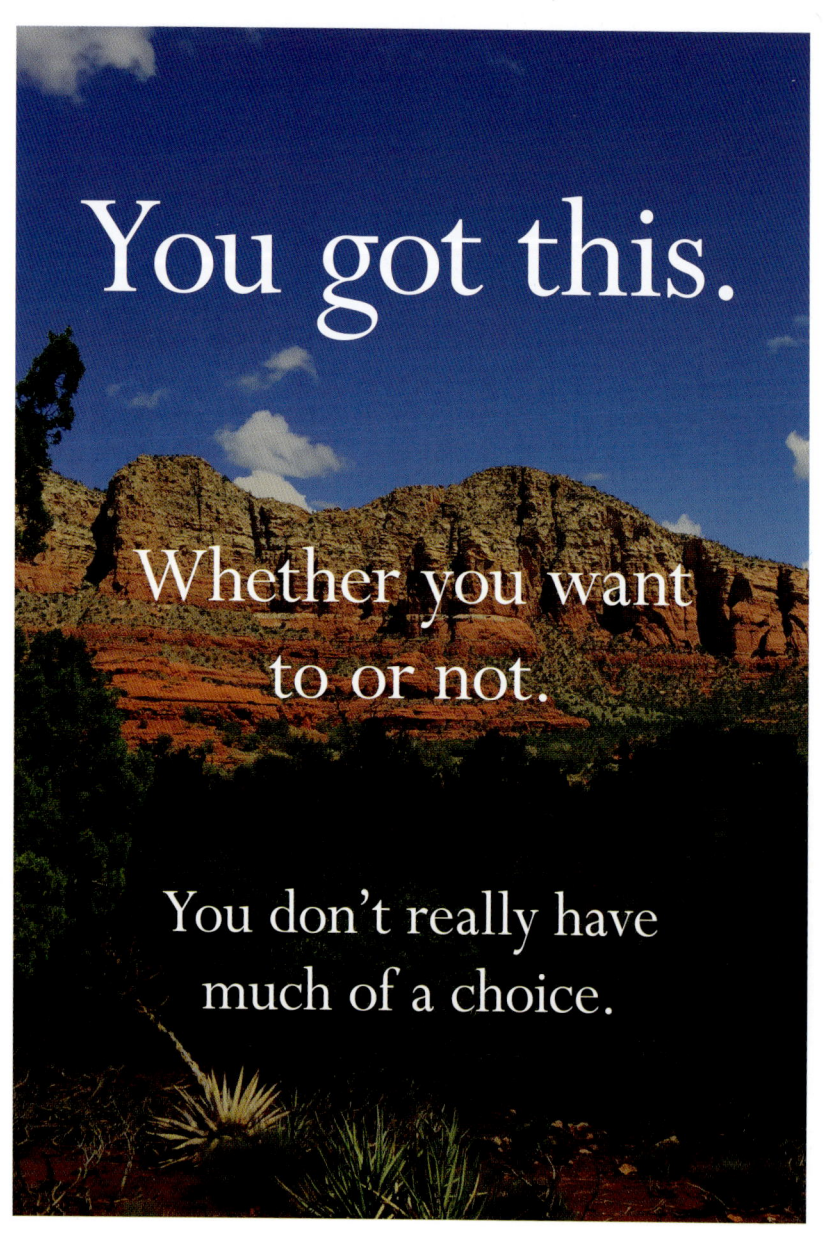

Whether you want to or not.

You don't really have much of a choice.

You are right where you need to be.

Working at a job you hate because food and housing and healthcare aren't free and you're massively in debt from buying things in desperate attempts to fill the void in your soul.

Is your name Sunday?

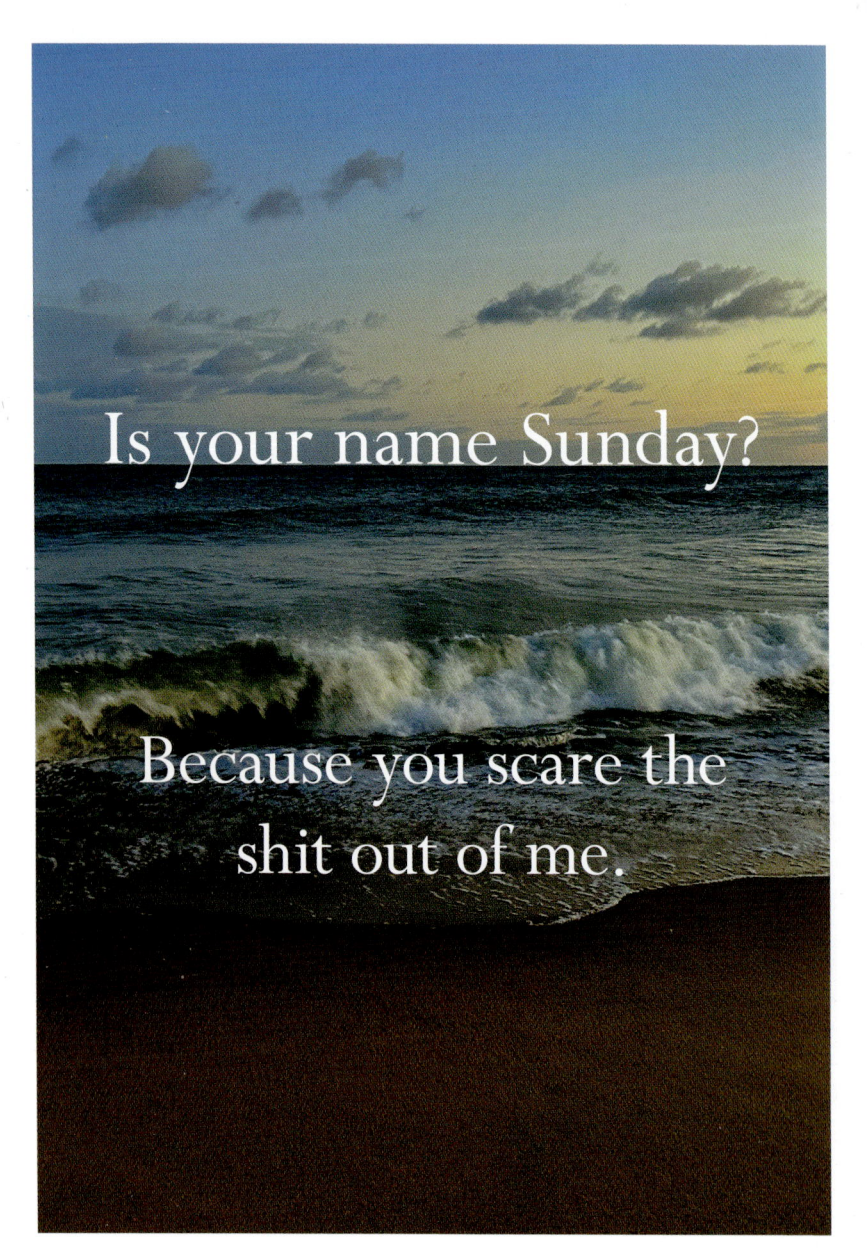

Because you scare the shit out of me.

Feeling trapped?

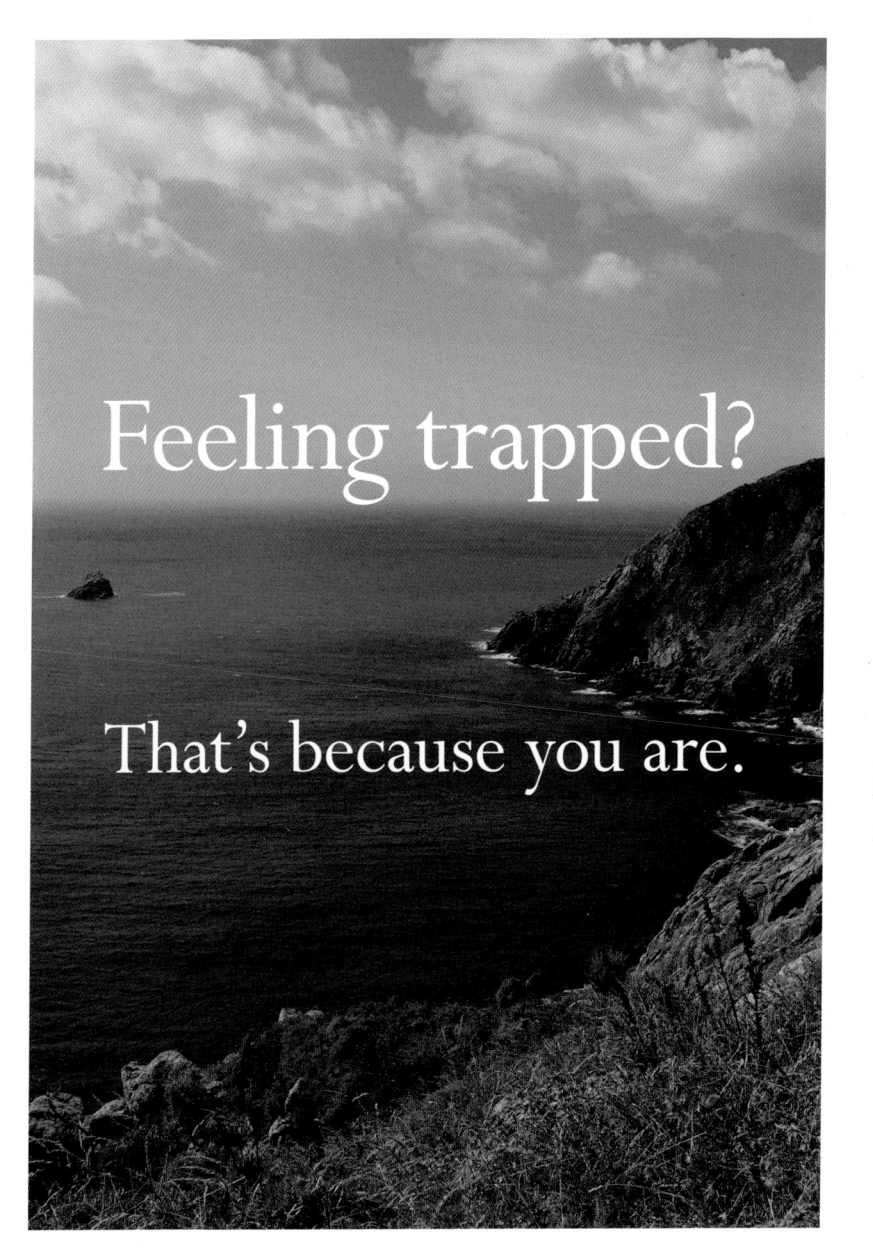

That's because you are.

I've feared work emails far more than I've ever feared death.

Act as if what you do truly matters.

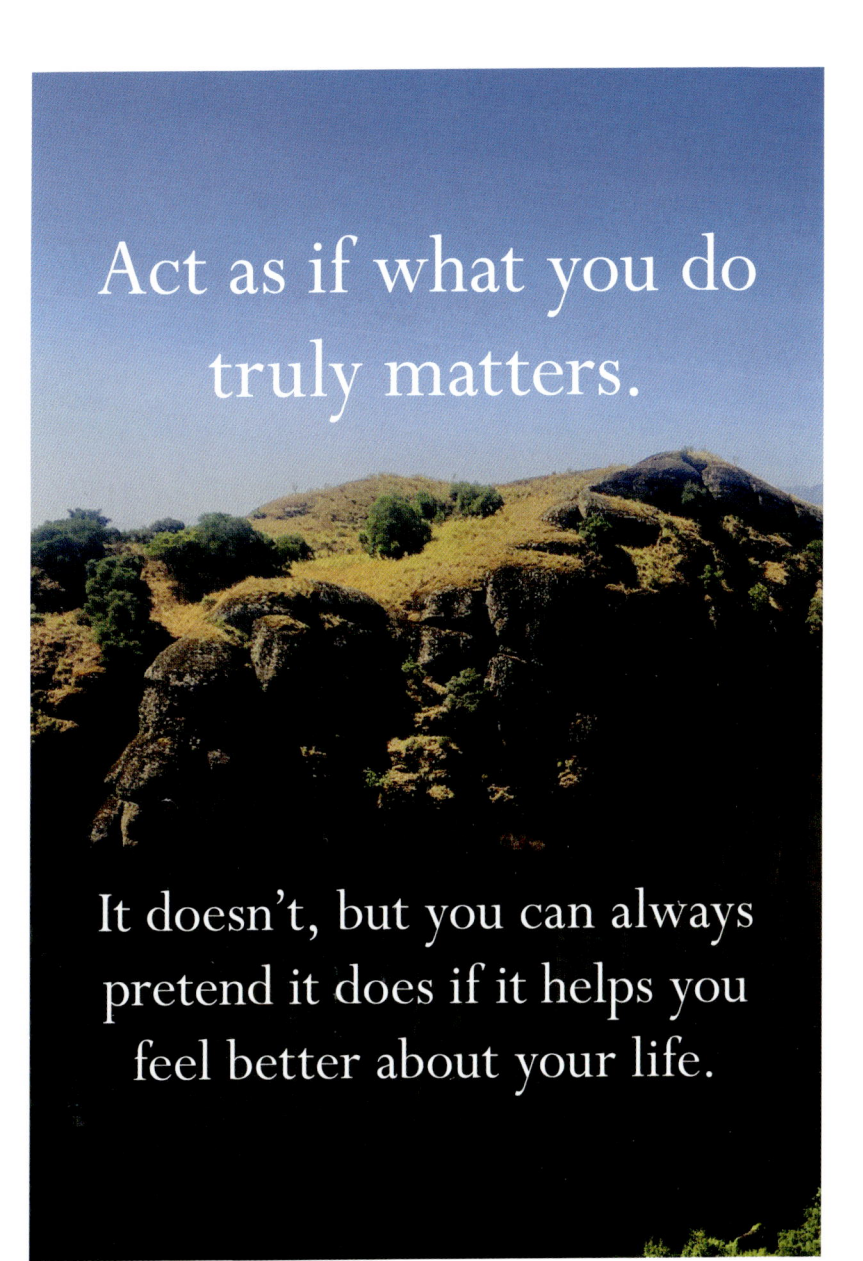

It doesn't, but you can always pretend it does if it helps you feel better about your life.

It's okay to cry.

Just do it where no one can see you.

Don't worry about work during your time off.

Get paid for your panic attacks.

Why finish something when you can just move on to another project that you'll never finish?

Stop obsessing so much over everything.

Instead, pick one thing and let it consume your every waking thought and haunt you in your sleep.

SUCCESS

Anything Can Be a Success

with the Right Reframing

What does success mean to you? Do you keep the bar low so that just getting by is a success? Or do you set it so high that you're never happy with anything? Do you set yourself up to fail by taking on more than you can handle? Or do you self-sabotage at any sign of success because you're afraid of it, and being a failure is comforting because it's familiar?

It's so strange how success can be the exact opposite of what we want. It's difficult to maintain day after day when we have it, whereas being a fuckup is quite simple. It's the path of least resistance. It's fair to say that I've been quite the success at fucking up my life over the years. And I just keep getting better at it.

Being happy? Completely off-brand. Being a complete fucking mess? That's my bag.

I feel least like a mess in those moments when I put others before myself. Being of service to others—yes, those other people I might not even want to be around—is the truest success I've had. It's what makes me feel like I'm not destined to be a fuckup.

Or not *just* a fuckup.

Stop wondering if you're good enough.

You're not.

You are filled with so much potential.

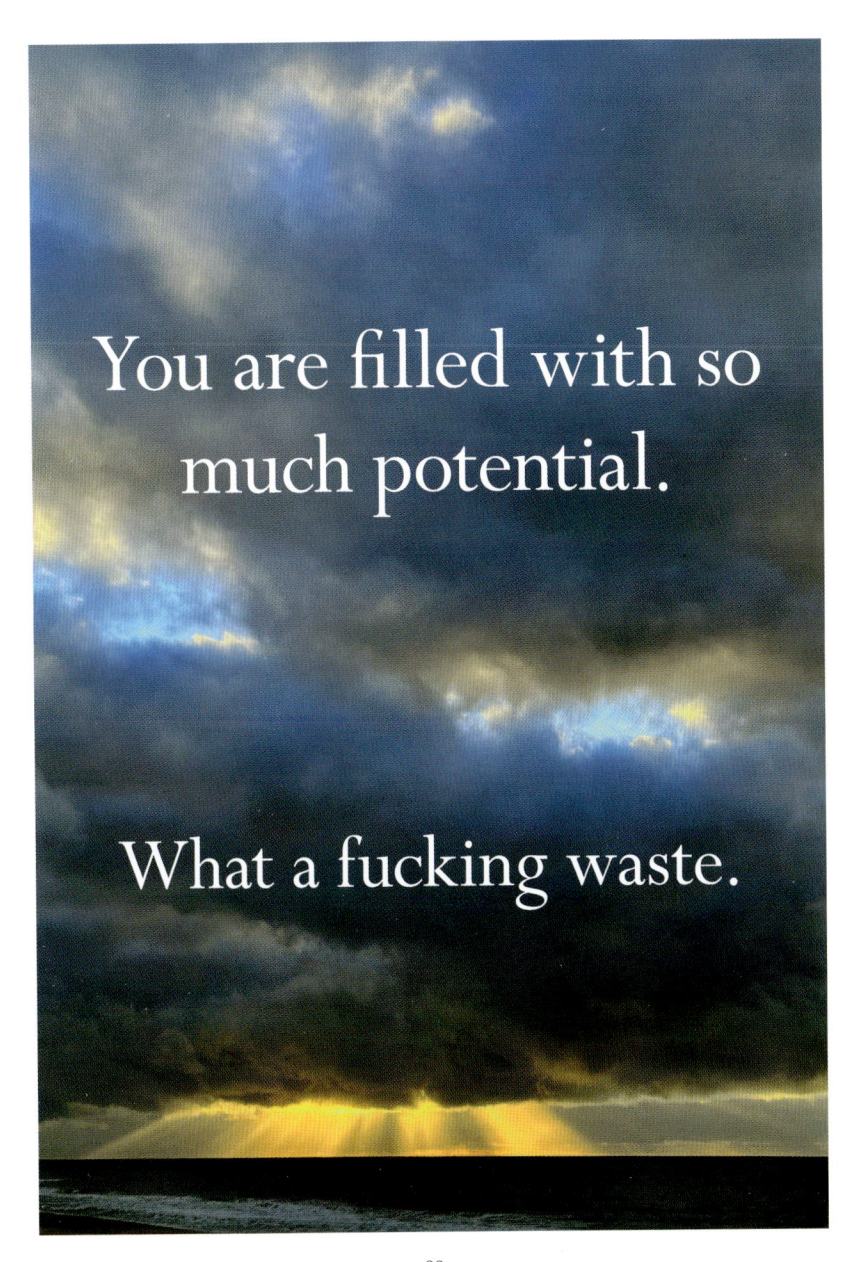

What a fucking waste.

Whatever you do, work at it with all your heart.

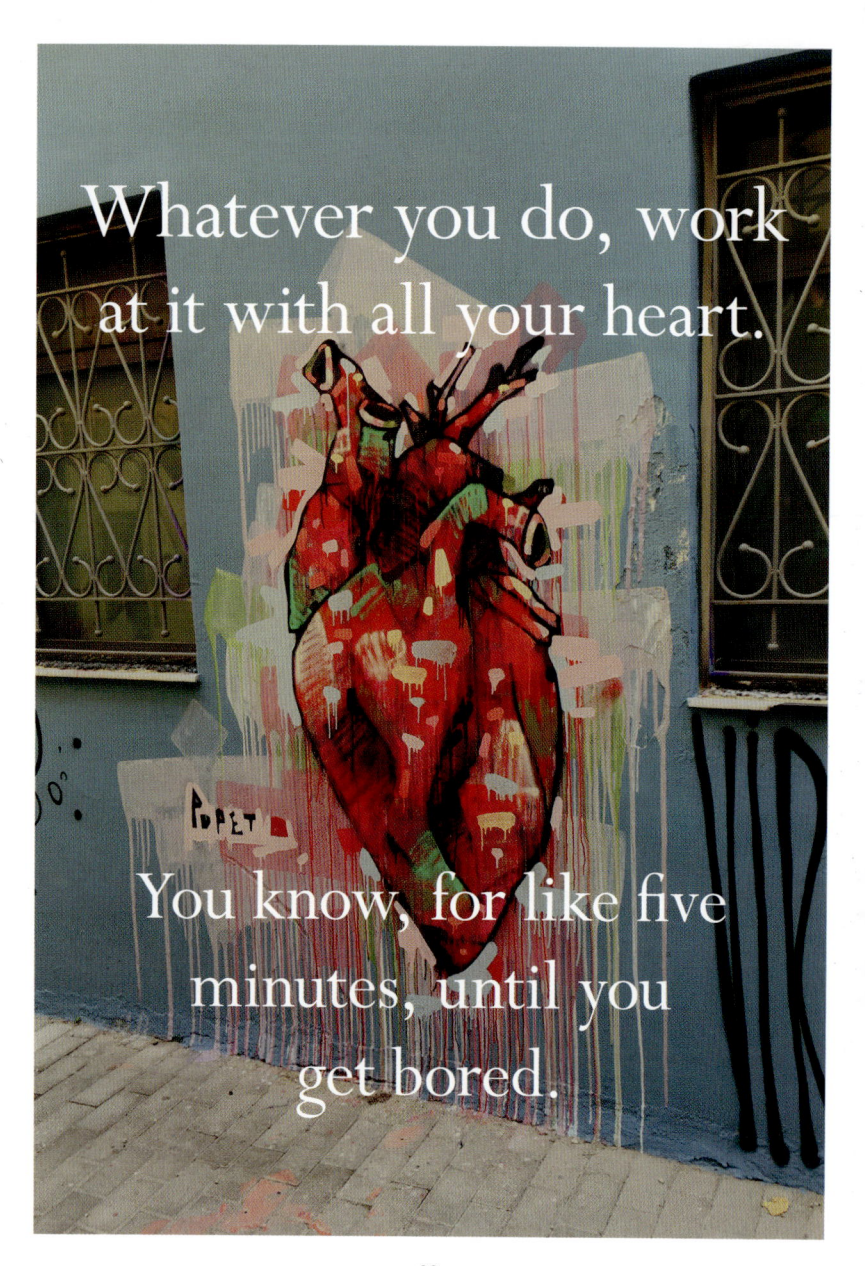

You know, for like five minutes, until you get bored.

Stop worrying about whether you're wasting your life.

You are.

You always have been.

Don't let what anyone thinks stop you from following your stupid dreams.

Believe in yourself.

There's nothing you can't fuck up.

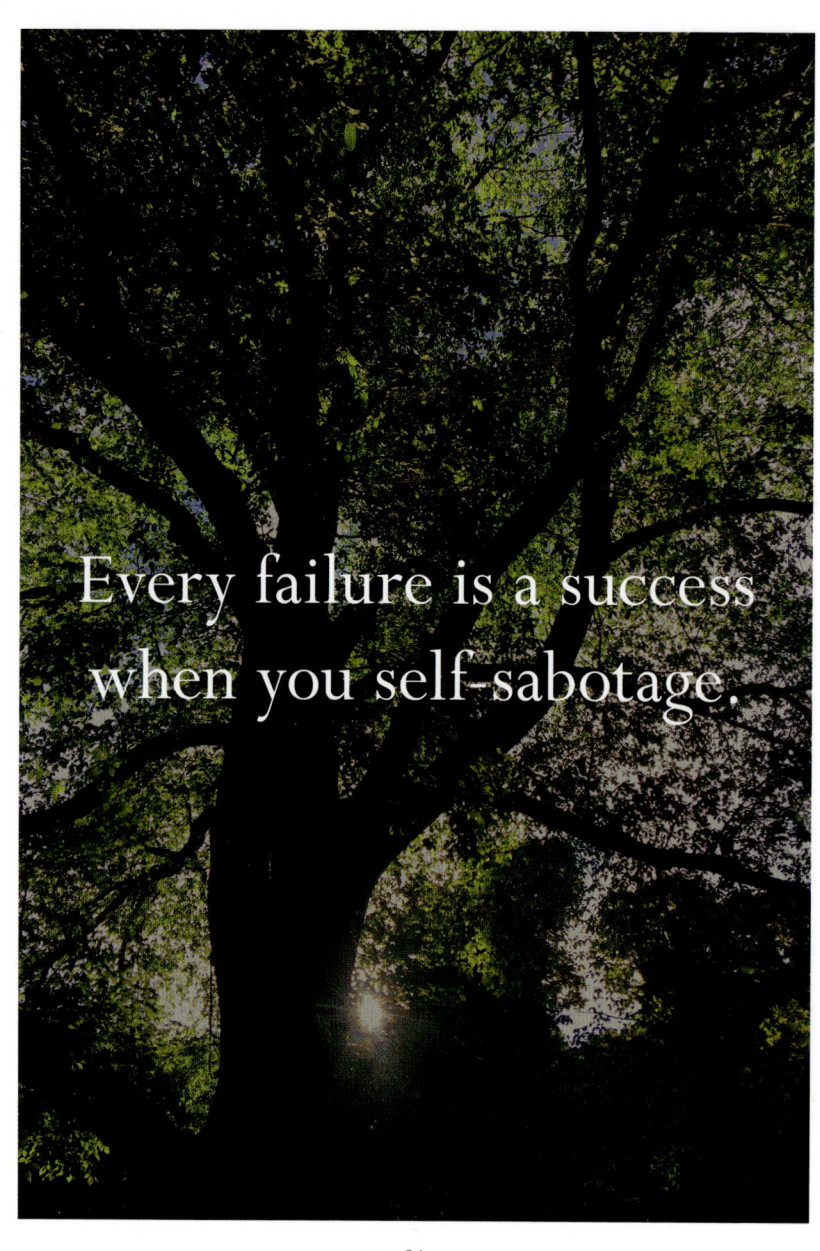

Every failure is a success when you self-sabotage.

Just don't.

You can't fail if you don't even try.

I am capable of making good decisions.

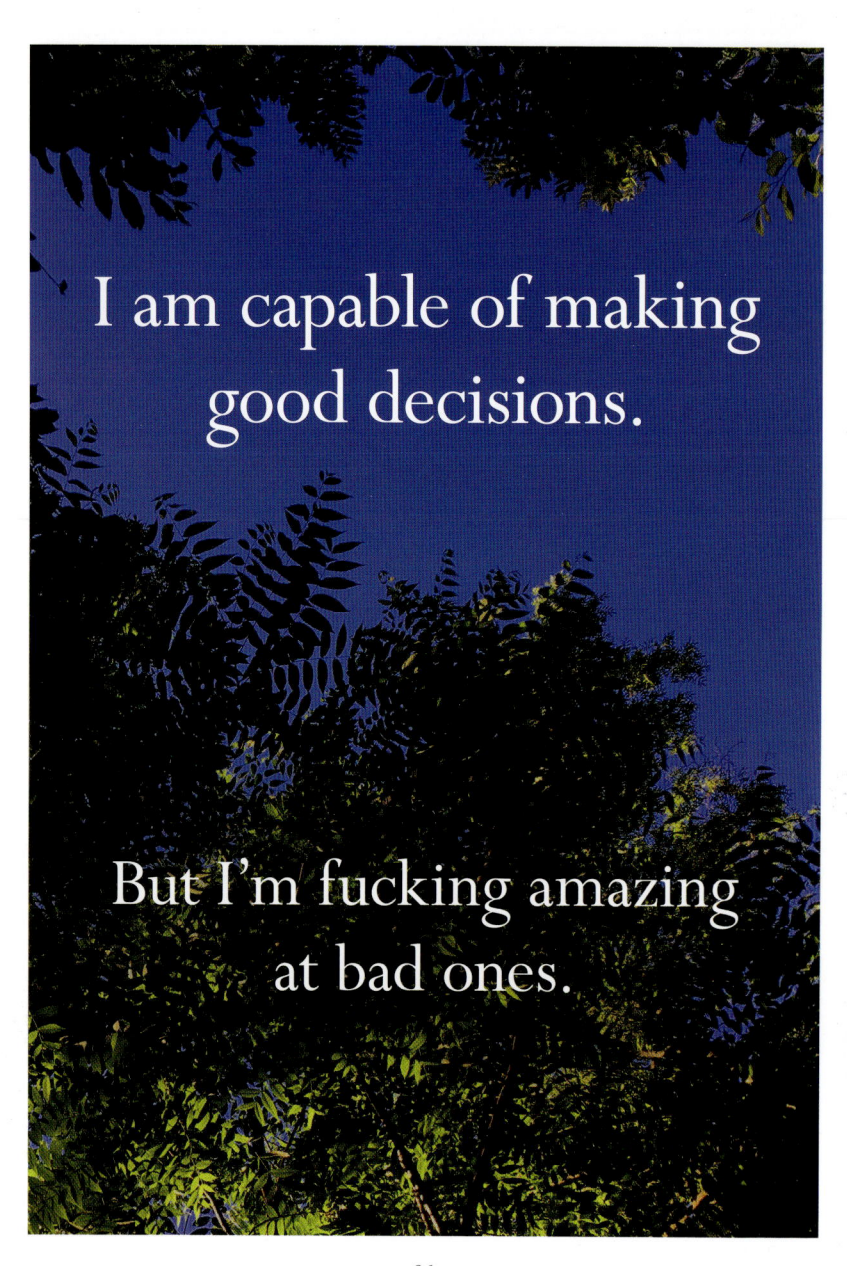

But I'm fucking amazing at bad ones.

Be proud of how far you've come.

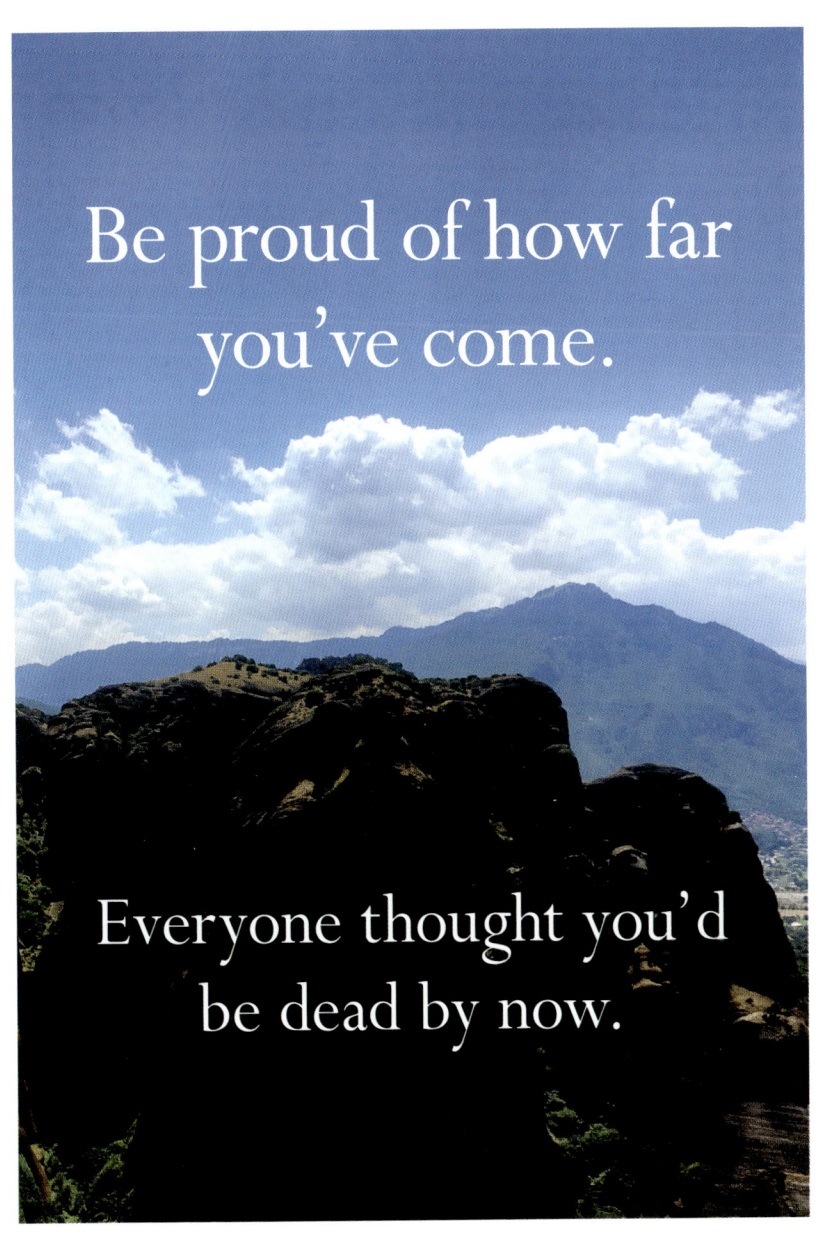

Everyone thought you'd be dead by now.

Just do whatever you want.

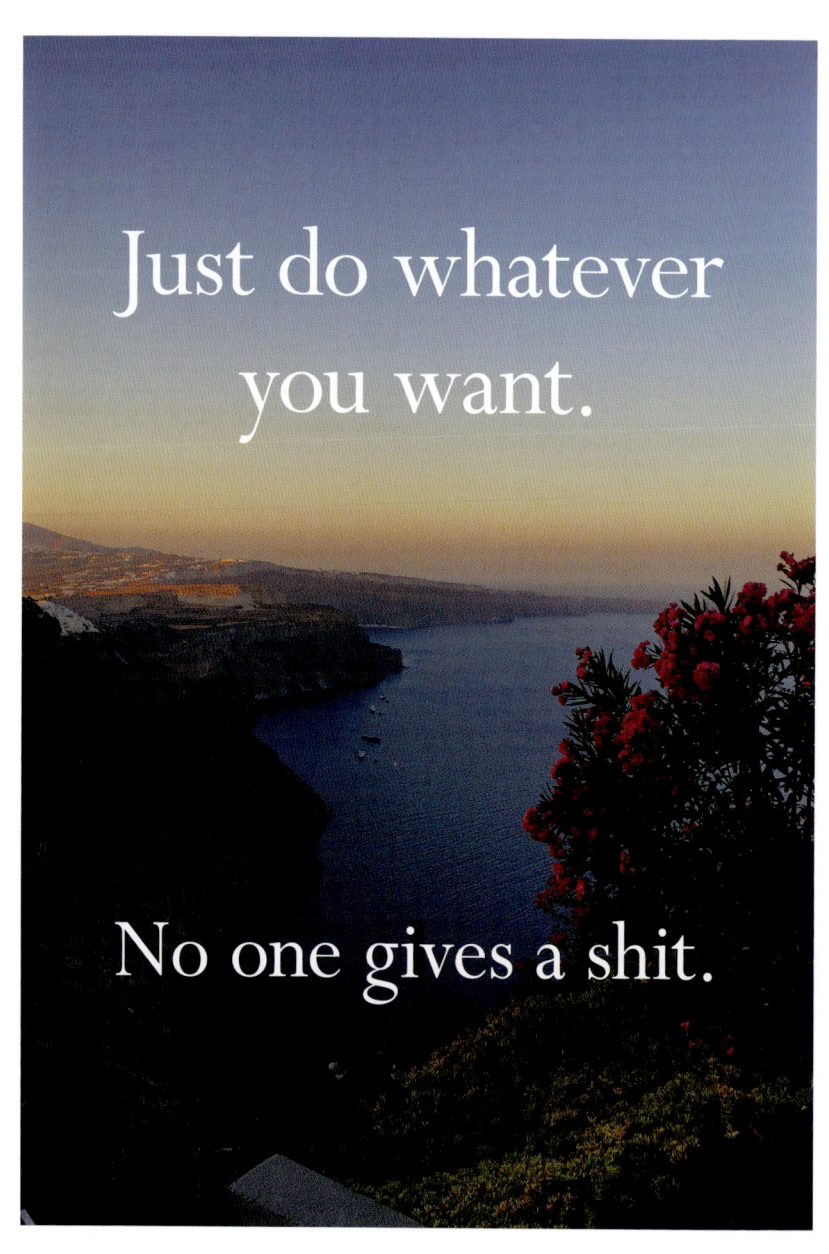

No one gives a shit.

It gets easier.

Eventually you just give up on your dreams, settle for what you have, and stop trying to be happy.

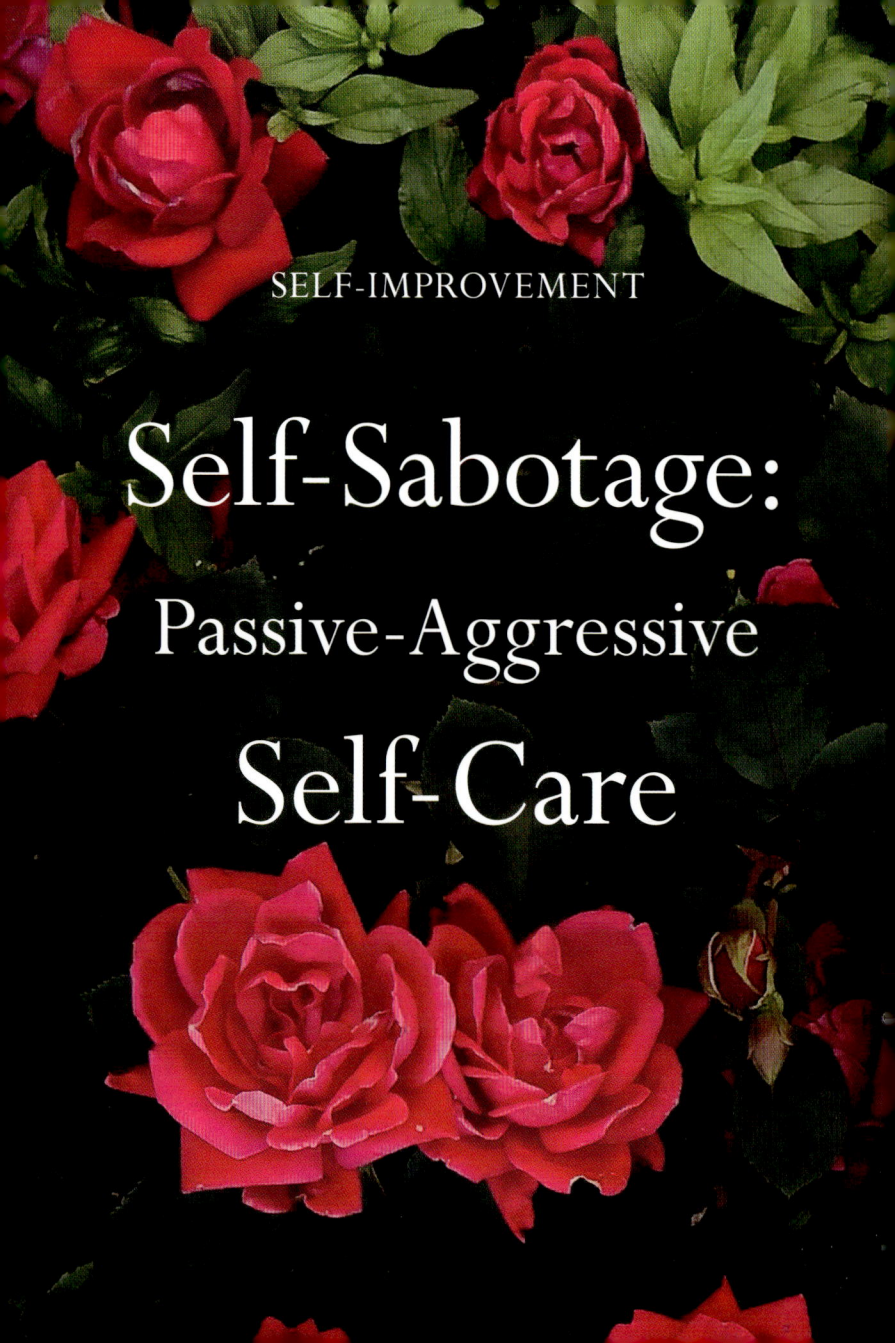

SELF-IMPROVEMENT

Self-Sabotage:

Passive-Aggressive

Self-Care

Take a look in the mirror. Do you like what you see?

Of course you don't! No one does. We're constantly disappointed with who we are. We need to exercise more. Eat better. Sleep better. Smile more. Think better. Be better. Everything we do is bad.

But those bad things feel so good! And it's the power that vices can hold over us that keeps us on the path of self-sabotage. Self-improvement is important, but self-destruction is much easier and more fun.

Change is rarely pleasant, and from what I've experienced over my years of living and working among other people, most of us would prefer to never even bother. If it ain't broke, fuck off. And if it is broke, fuck it.

The first step is to arrive at the idea that change is necessary all on our own—without the pesky pressure from other people. And to at least be self-aware about what needs fixing. You can't self-improve and self-sabotage at the same time.

Wait, sorry, I meant you can. I do it every day.

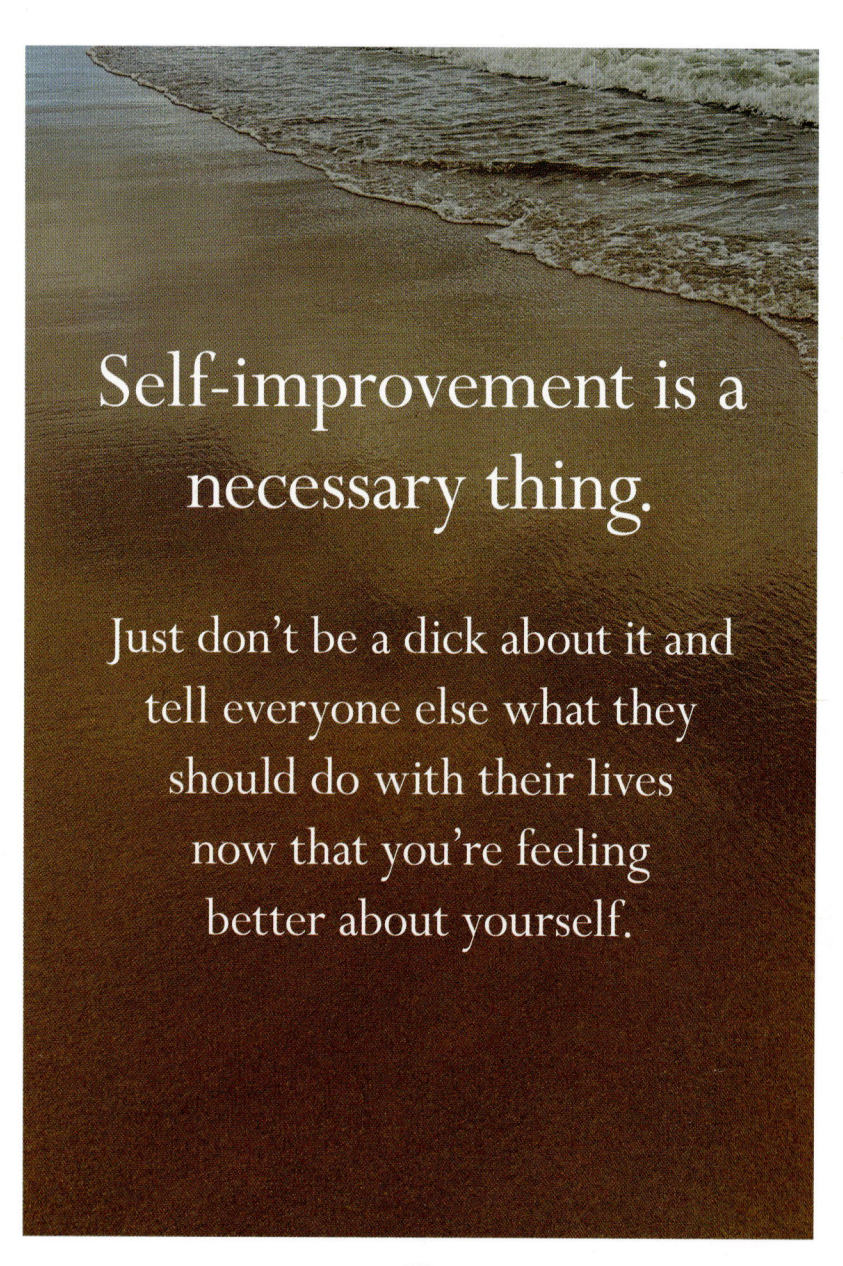

Self-improvement is a necessary thing.

Just don't be a dick about it and tell everyone else what they should do with their lives now that you're feeling better about yourself.

Only you have the power to change your life.

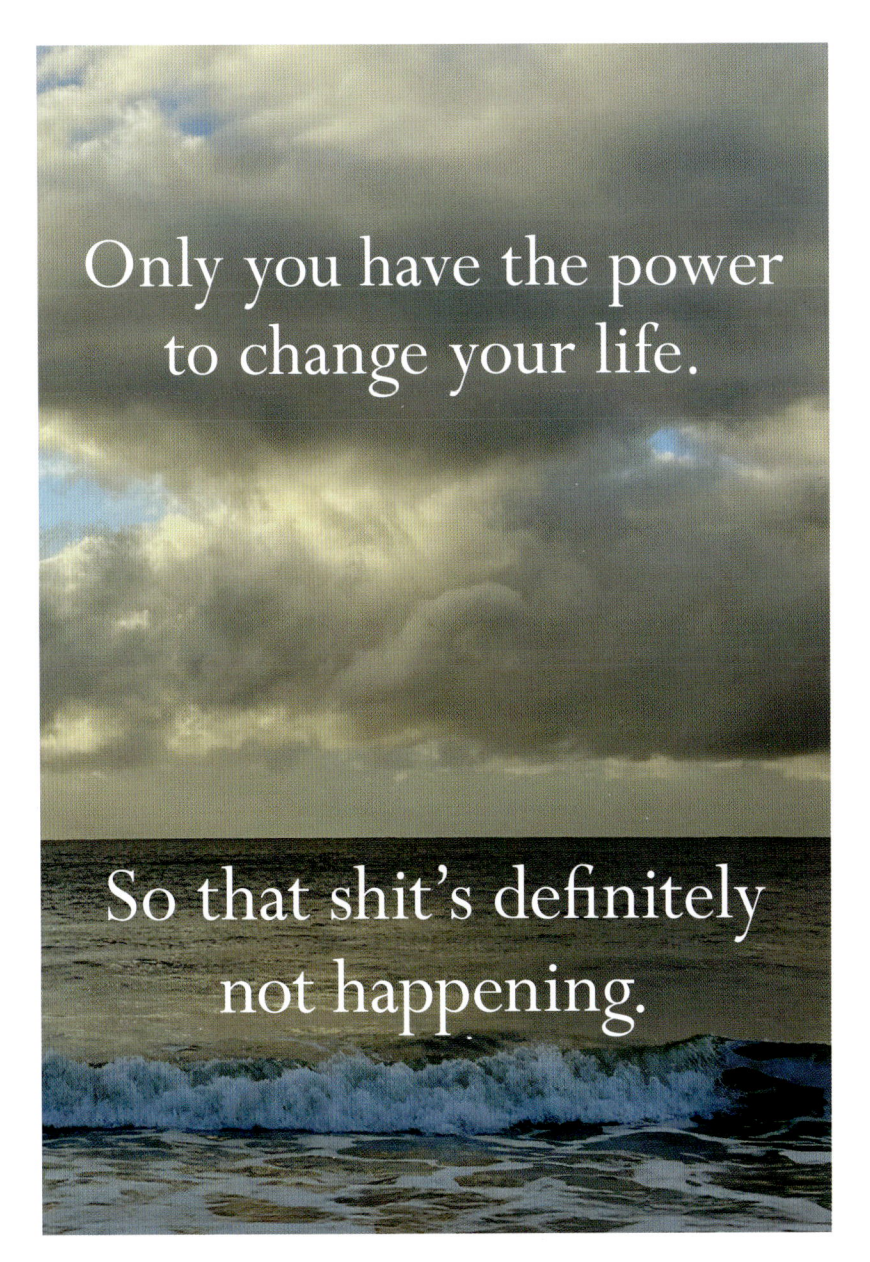

So that shit's definitely not happening.

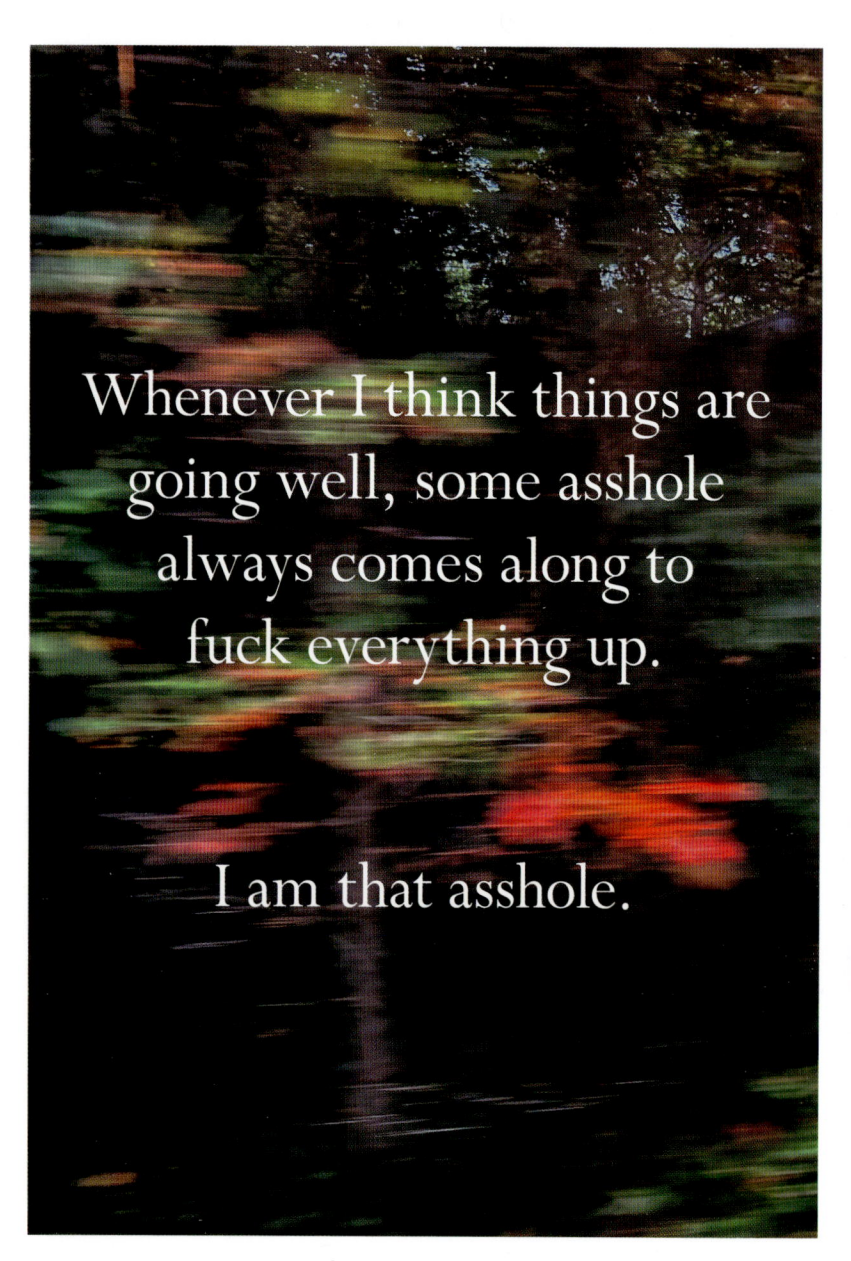

Whenever I think things are going well, some asshole always comes along to fuck everything up.

I am that asshole.

Don't be afraid to try new things.

Like lowering your expectations.

It's okay to walk away from things that are unhealthy for you.

Unfortunately, you can't walk away from yourself.

Today I will work on
not hating myself.

I will hate everyone
else instead.

Stop telling yourself the same old stories about how you suck.

You suck a lot more now.

Don't just be a fuckup.

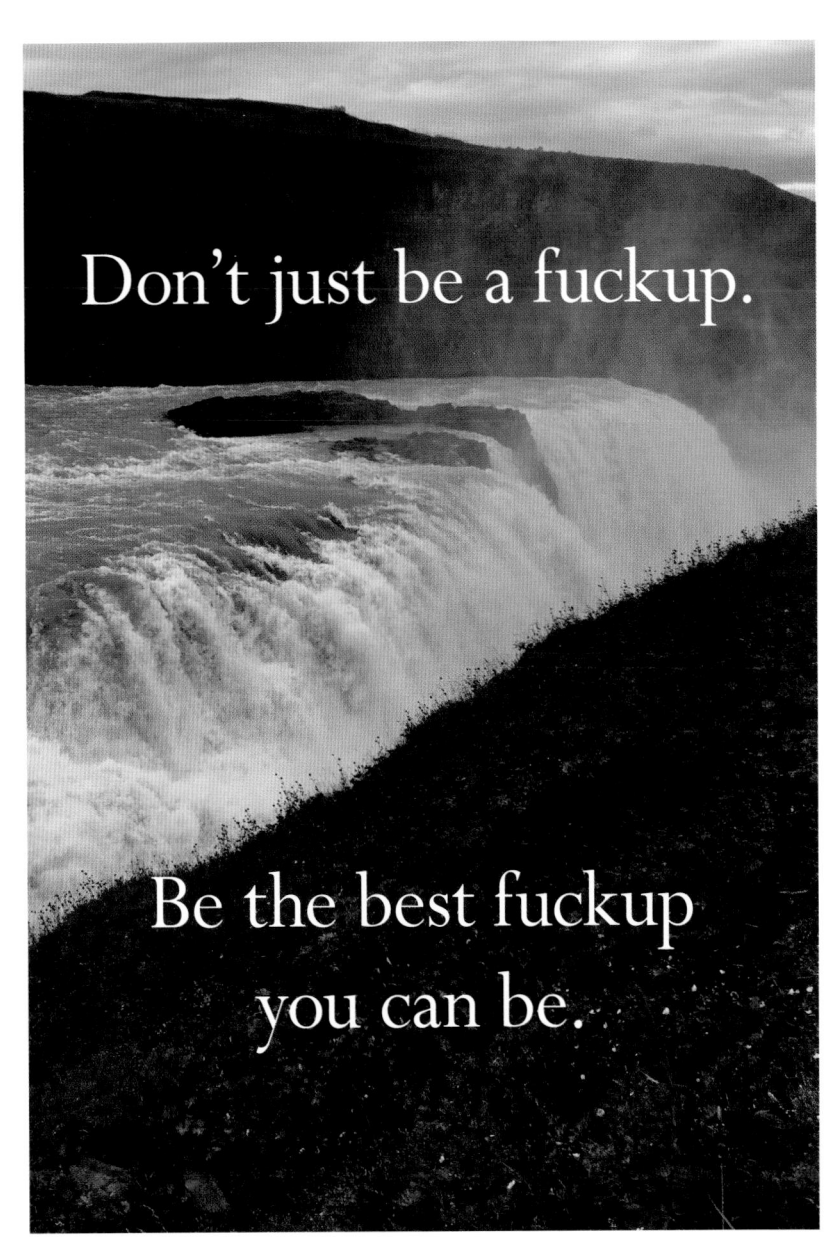

Be the best fuckup
you can be.

Today I will step out of my comfort zone.

Just to pick up something from the store, then I'm coming right back.

Be the change you want to see in the world.

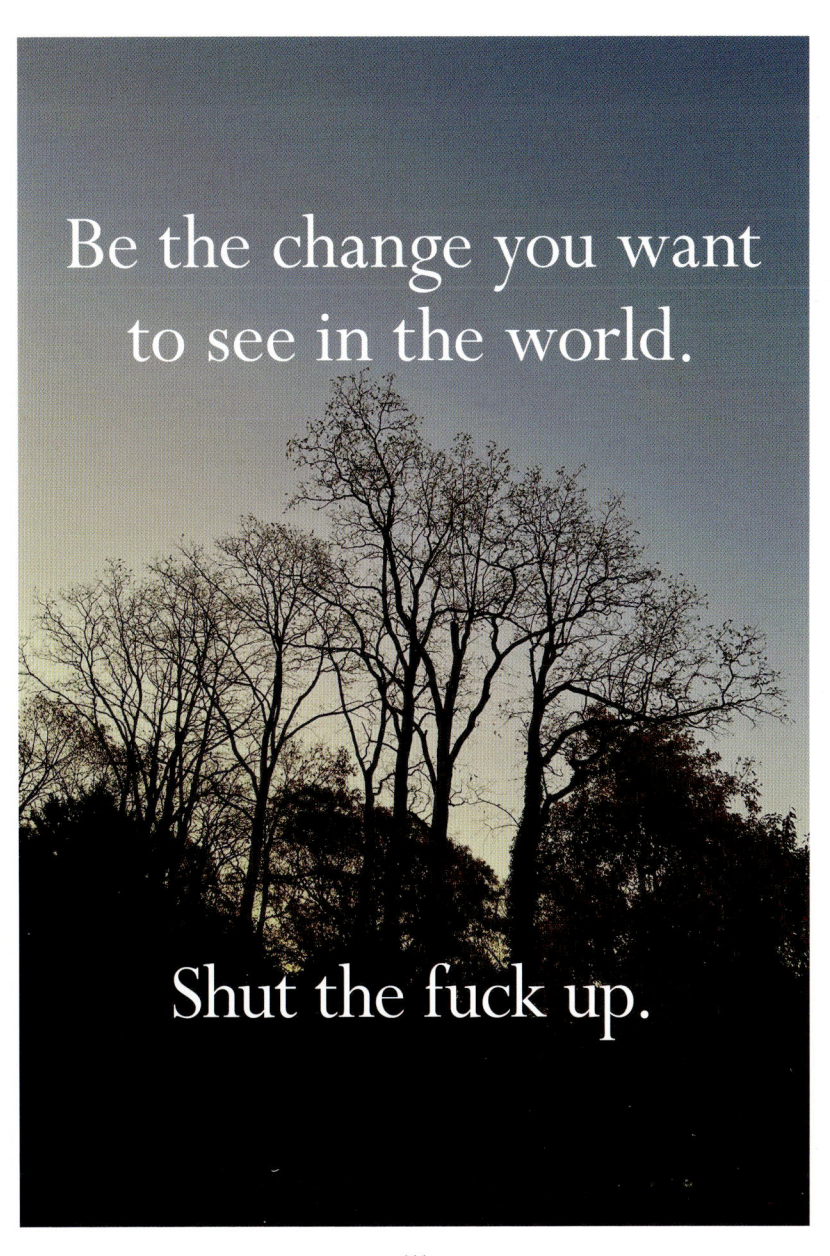

Shut the fuck up.

Stop beating yourself up over the mistakes you made in the past.

Instead, focus on making new, better mistakes in the future.

Sometimes it's necessary
to start over.

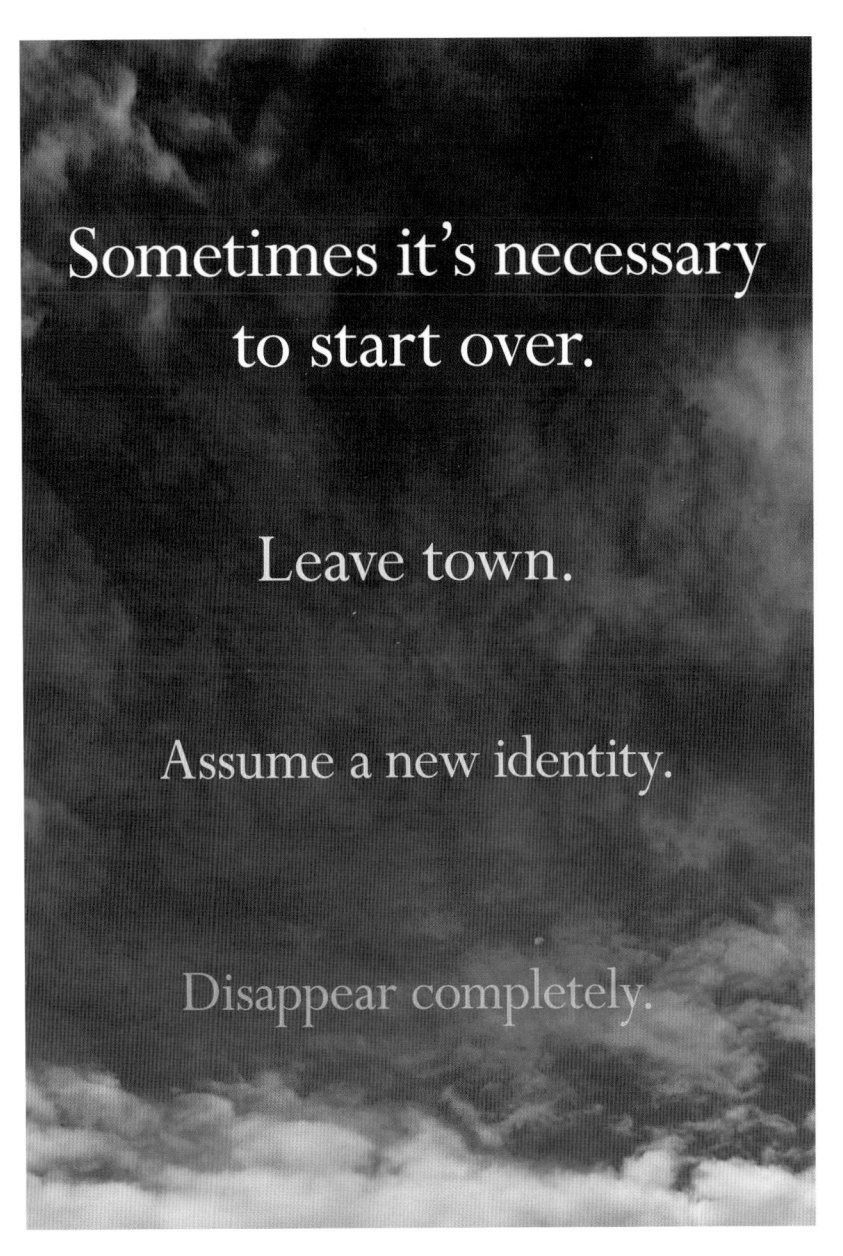

Leave town.

Assume a new identity.

Disappear completely.

GRIEF AND REGRET

Grief Takes as Long as It Has To

In the end, all we have are memories—those sweet moments with someone no longer with you because they either passed away or the relationship you once had with them is now just a ghost. And there are also the terrible moments—the ones that caused seismic shifts in our lives that haunted us for years. It's hard to tell which memories hurt the most: the ones when we were happy, or the ones when we lost that happiness.

Grief is one of the most unbearable of emotions. One of my therapists referred to it as "love with no place to go." It's the pain of the lack of light that someone once brought to your life. And the pain of not being able to share the love with them that you still feel.

And the worst part about grief is it works on its own timeline. One day you feel like things might be okay, the next you're waking up in tears from having experienced a fantasy in your head overnight that you'll never see fulfilled in real life. That shit can be excruciating. I've never experienced physical pain that rivaled grief.

But it does pass. It may never completely go away, but time and new memories dull the sharp edges of the old ones, and after a while you can begin to live again.

Just to make more horrendous life choices.

And on and on and on we go.

One day you're going to look back and ask yourself:

"What the actual fuck was I thinking?"

Or every day, depending on how much of a mess your life is.

I hate it when I wake up and realize I'm still me and nothing magically changed overnight.

It's okay to be sad.

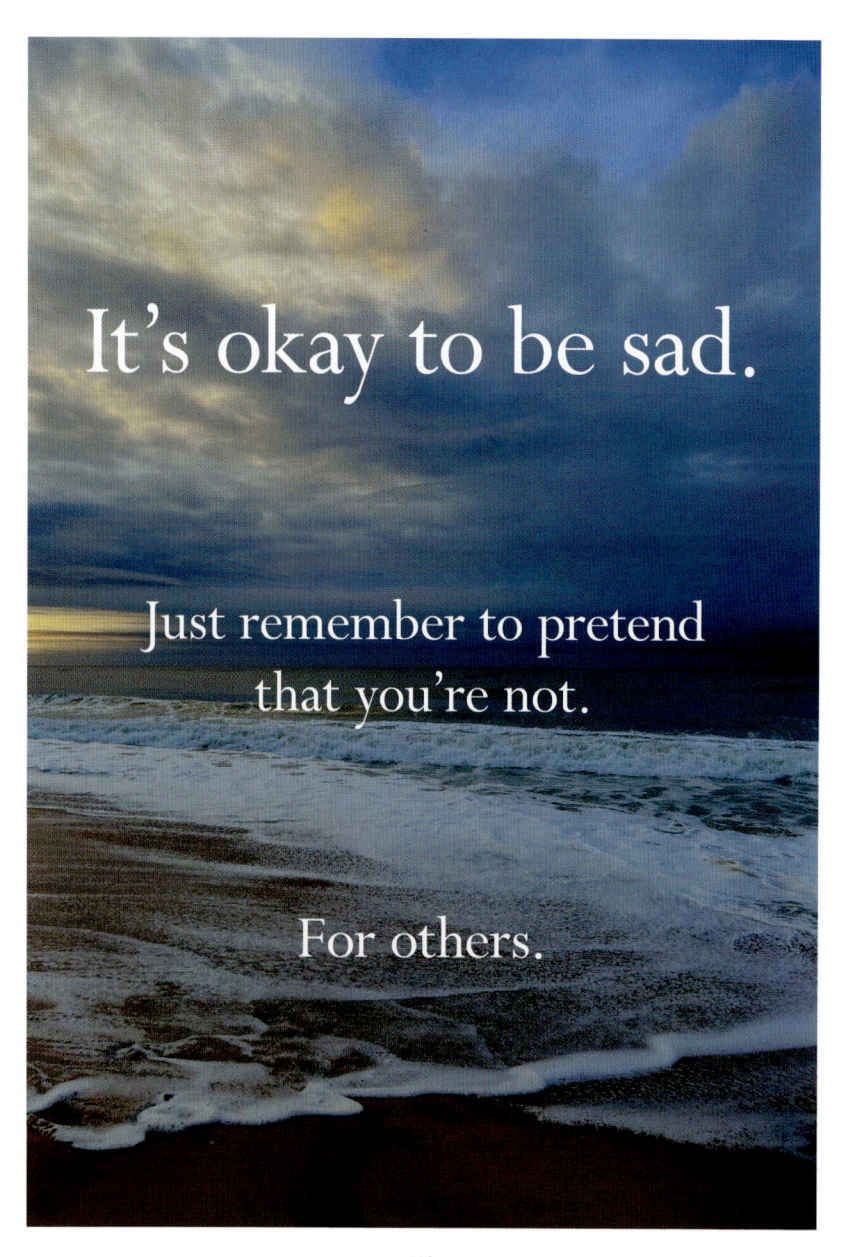

Just remember to pretend that you're not.

For others.

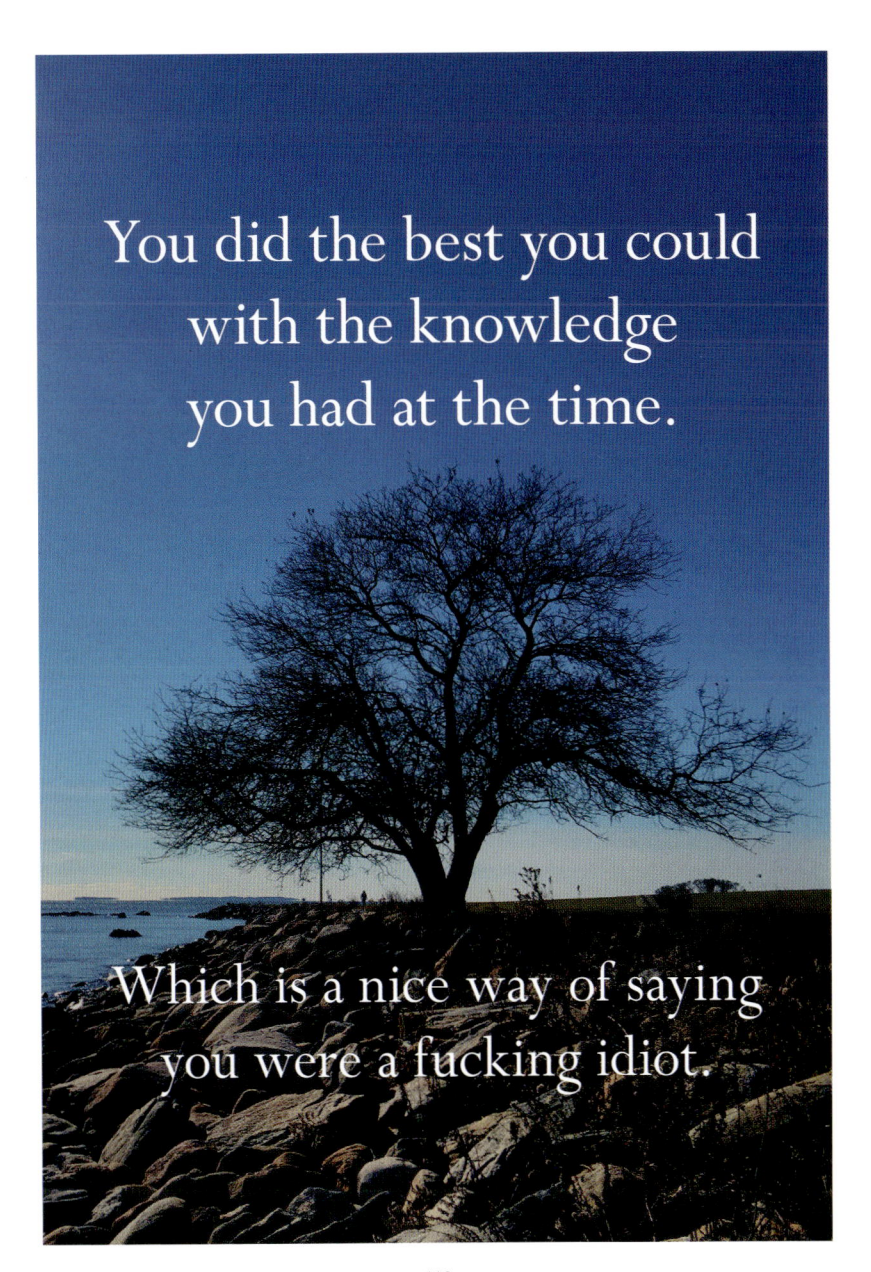

You did the best you could
with the knowledge
you had at the time.

Which is a nice way of saying
you were a fucking idiot.

Things didn't work out for a reason.

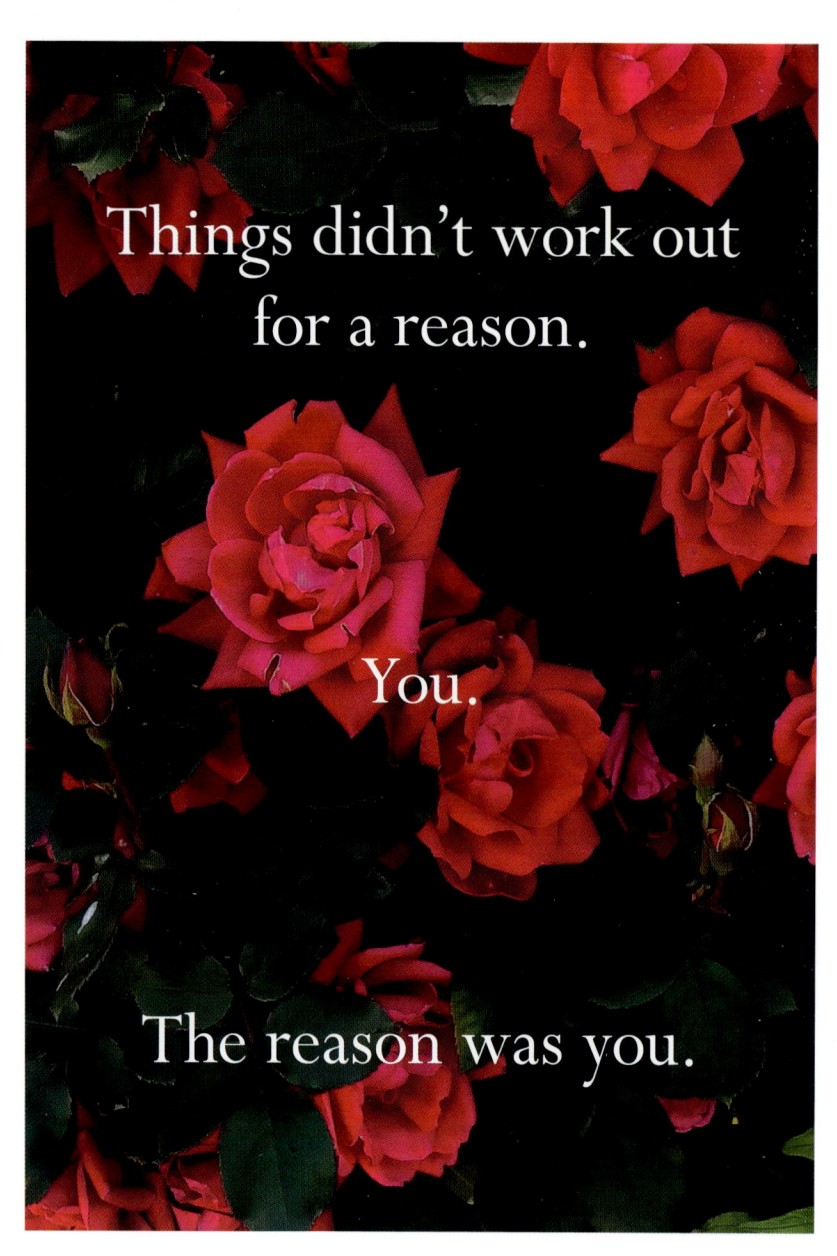

You.

The reason was you.

You still haven't met all of the people who are going to leave you.

Stop living in the past.

Seriously, your present self is a mess and needs your help.

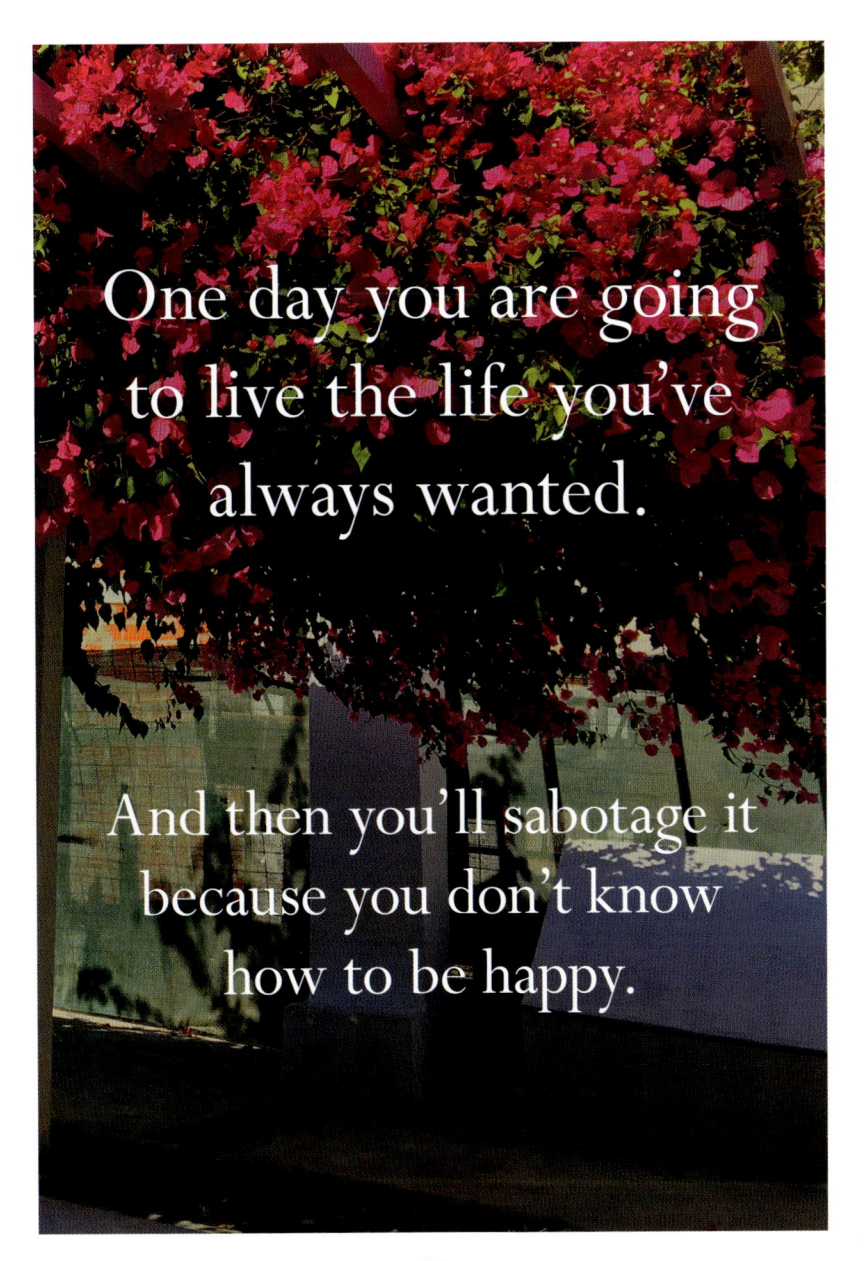

One day you are going
to live the life you've
always wanted.

And then you'll sabotage it
because you don't know
how to be happy.

Sometimes when things fall apart they're really falling into place.

Or so I tell myself after making things fall apart.

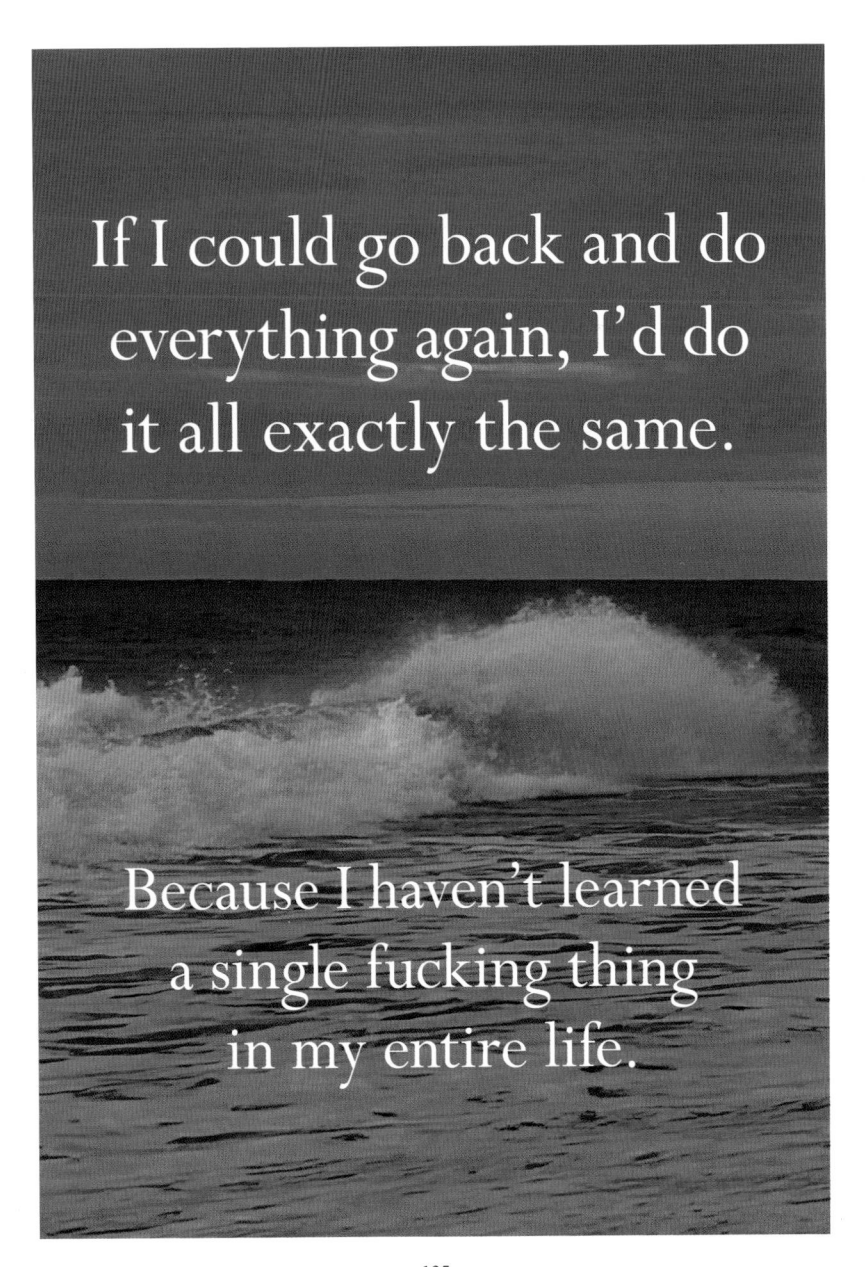

If I could go back and do everything again, I'd do it all exactly the same.

Because I haven't learned a single fucking thing in my entire life.

This too shall pass.

But what the fuck?

Everything will be okay.*

*Results may vary.

Acknowledgments

Thanks to Mom, Dad, Joe, Pete, Nancy, the Mikes, Jean, Gavin, Aidan, Declan, Lisa, Maria, Trisket, Bryan, Tiffe, Rich, Debbie, Dalila, Nat, Lin, Jerry, Albina, Maria V., Dave, Cherise, Wendy, Callie, Steve, Evelyn, Elora, Lynn, Michelle, Lauren, Brittany, Montauk Blue Hotel, and everyone else who supported me and helped create this book.